Praise for *Alignment*

"For those who give their all—and sometimes, more than their all—to their profession, this book offers a profoundly different perspective on 'work-life balance.'"
DANIEL WILLINGHAM, PhD, author of *Why Don't Students Like School?*

"The idea of 'work-life balance' never really worked for me, and Katie Keller Wood gets why. This is a thoughtful, compassionate, practical book for anyone who's tired of trying to balance the unbalanceable."
REBECCA JOINES SCHINSKY, chief of staff for Riot New Media Group

"*Alignment* is the book I wish every mission-driven professional could read before burnout ever takes hold. Katie Keller Wood offers a powerful reframe for those of us who care deeply about our work but also yearn to live with joy and wholeness."
DR. NICOLE-NOELLE EVANS, senior director of leadership at Embracing Equity

"Rarely does a book speak so fluently across professions: From oncology nurses to corporate leaders, the Montessori framing helps to contextualize the important role of work in our life's mosaic. The alignment of our mosaic is presented as fluid and evolving, making this a guide you'll return to repeatedly."
RUTH RIVIERE, senior corporate leader

"A compassionate, thoughtful guide for those of us who love our work but are done with the myth of 'balance.' If you're craving a more sustainable, meaningful way of living—a life in which all of you is allowed to show up—*Alignment* is the book you didn't know you needed."
AMY PORT, co-founder of Heroic Public Speaking

"As a former 'Montessori kid,' *Alignment* is not just a revelation; it is a homecoming. Katie Keller Wood shows us how to finally let go of the impossible task—achieving 'work-life balance'—and redirect our focus to our cosmic task, in a way that supports us as a whole person."
AJ HARPER, author of *Write a Must-Read*

"This must-read book is a lifeline for mission-driven souls seeking a new way forward that honors purpose and personal well-being. Transformative, tender, and urgently needed."
SUSIE DEVILLE, award-winning author of *Buoyant*

"Combining research with story, Katie Keller Wood draws us in to reevaluate how we think about work. *Alignment* is full of tools, prompts, and guidance for immediate implementation, bringing the reader through changes and into alignment as they move through the pages."
ELIZABETH SLADE, founder and executive director of Public Montessori in Action International

"If you've ever felt the pressure to compartmentalize who you are in order to succeed, *Alignment* offers more than just permission to bring your whole self—it offers a process. For values-driven leaders, this book is a call to realign—not just to function, but to flourish."

TRICIA MONTALVO TIMM, award-winning author of *Embrace the Power of You*

"Katie Keller Wood's *Alignment* is a blueprint for purposeful living with respect (for self and others) at its core."

GENA COX, PhD, author of *Leading Inclusion*

"This book captivated me. It's a refreshing take that invites you to reimagine your life as a mosaic, where all the pieces support each other. A must-read for anyone ready to live and work with more freedom, intention, and heart."

LINDA CAREY, co-founder of the Tutu Project and president of the Carey Foundation

"Katie Keller Wood reminds us that we matter in not just what we do but who we are, and that our work and our lives do not have to be in constant battle, but can be woven together in a beautiful, living mosaic."

TATENDA BLESSING MUCHIRIRI, founder and chief dreamer of Montessori on Wheels

"Drawing from Montessori's radical view that work is not the opposite of play but a pathway to self-discovery, this book offers an outstanding mosaic model that honors both your mission and your humanity. It's a guide for thriving—not just succeeding—in a life of passionate work."

JEFFREY SHAW, author of *The Self-Employed Life, Lingo,* and *Sell to the Rich*

"*Alignment* is an outstanding primer on how to align your whole (meaning your work and nonwork) life. My advice? Get her book. Jump into the chapters. Do the exercises (yes, actually do them!). And then when you feel you are out of alignment again, repeat."

CAROL GUNN, MD, occupational medicine physician, patient advocate, speaker

"If your work is purposeful and you've ever felt consumed by it, *Alignment* is a must-read. This book is especially powerful for those of us in healthcare and human services, where the line between mission and overextension can blur fast. It's not about balance; it's about wholeness."

DEBORAH BAKTI, author of *Now What?* and host of *The Relational Approach* podcast

"Katie Keller Wood helps to give readers a sense that the mosaic of their alignment can be achieved when the chaos of imbalance is recognized. This is an easy-to-read, thought-provoking book that has been sculpted to celebrate and support changes in mindset."

EDY NATHAN, author of *It's Grief*

"Through compelling stories and guided practice, Katie Keller Wood shows how Montessori principles can be used to align your personal life and career, to better meet your goals, and to meet the need for connection and work that every human shares. This book will change lives."

TRISHA THOMPSON-WILLINGHAM, MEd, Montessori consultant, co-founder of the Virginia Montessori Association

ALIGNMENT

ALIGNMENT

A Montessori Approach
to Reimagining
Work-Life Balance

KATIE KELLER WOOD

Copyright © 2025 by Katie Keller Wood

All rights reserved. No part of this book may be reproduced, stored in a retrieval system or transmitted, in any form or by any means, without the prior written consent of the publisher or a license from The Canadian Copyright Licensing Agency (Access Copyright). For a copyright license, visit accesscopyright.ca or call toll free to 1-800-893-5777.

Cataloguing in publication information is available from Library and Archives Canada.
ISBN 978-1-77458-485-9 (paperback)
ISBN 978-1-77458-486-6 (ebook)

Page Two
pagetwo.com

Page Two™ is a trademark owned by Page Two Strategies Inc., and is used under license by authorized licensees

Cover and interior design by Jennifer Lum
Printed and bound in Canada by Friesens
Distributed in Canada by Raincoast Books
Distributed in the US and internationally by Macmillan

25 26 27 28 29   5 4 3 2 1

katiekellerwood.com

For everyone whose work helps move the needle towards a more beautiful, more peaceful, more just world. Your work matters. And you matter more.

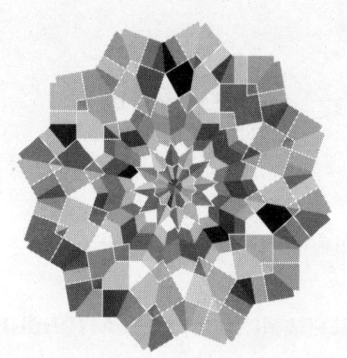

Contents

Author's Note *1*

PART ONE **REFRAMING OUR RELATIONSHIP WITH WORK**
Out of Balance, Into Alignment

1. Work-Life Balance Is a Lie: Crafting Your Life Mosaic *5*
2. Let's Face It, Our Work Is Personal (And That's Okay!) *31*
3. You Don't Have to Quit Your Job (But You Might Want To) *57*
4. Finding Alignment, Part I: Noticing Our Work-Life Alliance *77*
5. Finding Alignment, Part II: Addressing Misalignment *95*

PART TWO **SUPPORTING A HEALTHY ALLIANCE**
Aligning and Realigning

6 Expanding Your Mosaic:
Montessori for Adult Development *115*

7 Honoring Our Alignment:
A Montessori Approach to Time,
Boundaries, and Negotiation *129*

8 Our Ever-Changing Mosaics:
Navigating Change and Grief *149*

9 Your Alignment Matters:
Our Interconnected Mosaics *167*

Acknowledgments *175*

Notes *177*

Author's Note

NAMES AND IDENTIFYING DETAILS of some individuals in this work have been changed to respect their privacy. Some story details may have also been adapted or altered for clarity, narrative flow, or to account for the natural imperfections of memory. These adjustments are intended to illuminate the broader themes of this book and should not be interpreted as misrepresentation.

This book, while I hope helpful to people doing important work in the world, is not designed to treat or manage clinical needs and should not be seen as a substitute for professional or therapeutic support. The opinions and approaches I recommend are my own, and I write not as a mental health professional, but as a teacher and guide.

I have tried to use language throughout this text that is inclusive, to honor the full humanity of each individual. I recognize, too, that language and related understandings of what is inclusive, helpful, or supportive can and do change over time and among cultures, and I will always be learning more.

PART 1

REFRAMING OUR RELATIONSHIP WITH WORK

Out of Balance, Into Alignment

1

Work-Life Balance Is a Lie: Crafting Your Life Mosaic

I REMEMBER THE FIRST TIME my husband, Jonathan, gave me "the talk."

"I'm telling you this because I love you."

My stomach dropped. I took a breath and turned from the counters to face him sitting at the kitchen table.

"And I want to support your work, because I know how much it means to you. But I'm worried."

Just breathe, I reminded myself. I pulled up the other chair and sat at the kitchen table with him.

"You're keeping crazy hours and seem so stressed. You always say that 'next week will be better,' once you get through whatever this current thing is, but next week is never better!"

He's the most even-keeled person I know, but I could hear the hurt creeping into his voice.

I stayed quiet to give him my attention.

"We plan date nights, but you fall asleep thirty minutes into the movie. We spend most of the dinner hour processing the emotions of whatever happened during the day. You're more irritable than normal. This just doesn't feel sustainable."

The defensiveness pricked up inside me as I tried to consider his concerns. *Is that really true? Surely he's exaggerating a bit. Well, maybe, but doesn't he understand that people are counting on me? What am I supposed to do? I can't just abandon them! And anyway, didn't we just recently do that fun thing together...*

"And I miss you."

Oof.

I could see that he was right.

We took some time that night to discuss the things that mattered most to both of us, and I made my very first "better balance plan." Maybe you've made one? You know, where you figure out exactly how it is you're going to solve this problem and find more "balance" between your work and your life? To try and resolve, once and for all, the excruciating tension you feel between the work that matters to you and all the important nonwork parts of your life?

That night I stayed at the kitchen table for a while to think it all through. I had already admitted Jonathan was right; I had been surviving day to day at work for a while now, and I was no longer a new teacher. Sure, when you're learning the ropes, when you're developing all your content from scratch, things just take longer. But I was well past those days, so something had to give if this was going to be a sustainable career. I was confident that this better balance plan would be the key. (And if there is one thing I love, it is a good plan!) So I carefully calculated my responsibilities and put time estimates with each one. I reviewed my contract and additional responsibilities I held. And like anyone who has made an overly optimistic budget, I was sure that with some simple planning the resources allocated could match the needs and demands.

Maybe you've had "the talk" too, where loved ones express concern that we seem to be losing ourselves in our work. When they're worried about and sometimes even hurt by the ways that we give everything we can to the work and come home empty. Maybe no one has had to give you the talk, because you've recognized this problem in yourself! Maybe you've created one (or a hundred) better balance plans yourself. Or maybe you're trying to help someone else, someone who loves their work but struggles to feel that they have, that they are, enough. We become desperate for another way.

Many of us serve in the so-called "helping" professions—as teachers, nurses, lawyers, community organizers, social workers—but all of us see our work as part of our contribution to making the world a better place. We often choose these occupations because of the meaning they bring to our lives. Because we have something important to offer. Whether we are drawn to our professions as a kind of calling or simply as one way to make our world a better place for now, we feel that we're here for a reason. We're satisfied that we've chosen the path that feels right for us.

But then, something happens along the way. Despite warnings of burnout, and admonitions to keep a healthy work-life balance, we can find ourselves being consumed by our work. I've heard the stories, and even lived some of them:

- The healthcare worker who needs to spend as much time recovering from her shifts as she did working them.

- The teacher spending more than seventy hours a week on work, just to feel that he was still performing at only an adequate (or even sub-par) level.

- The social worker who worries constantly about their clients, whether or not they're "off."

- The nonprofit director or small business owner of a mission-driven organization, waking up earlier and earlier, spending weekends and holidays, trying to find a way to keep all the balls in the air to meet the endless needs that their organization is supposed to serve.

Then we feel bad. We know our work has taken over, and we're missing important connections with ourselves, our families, our friends. We vow to strive for "better balance," even as we're flirting dangerously with (or completely crossed over into) burnout.

It took me years to recognize, but the irony of my better balance plan (and the many that followed) was that my primary strategy for increasing joy and connection in my life was to box myself in. The only solution I could see was to give myself more rules, which of course meant more things to feel bad about when I couldn't measure up. I had rules about when and how I was "allowed" to work, including when to get to work, leave work, check email, or even talk about work! But all these rules just increased my inner turmoil, since they only made me feel more guilty. Either I was following my plan, which meant sometimes arbitrarily and artificially closing the door on work that mattered to me, or I was "cheating" on my plan by thinking about or engaging in my work during my time off.

I was also trying to implement my better balance plan without any contingencies. I had no strategy for when the conflicts would inevitably arise, the unexpected demands on my time and attention. I had no framework for making decisions, no way of knowing how to prioritize the different parts of myself. I had no tactic for managing my emotions around work that sometimes or often felt overwhelming. And perhaps worst of all, I had no way to calibrate, to recognize when I had allowed other people's priorities to dictate my time and energy, rather than fully owning my choices.

And while that's all terrible in retrospect, I might have been able to carry on if *any* of the better balance plans I made had actually worked. But they never did! Despite my sincere efforts, like a waning full moon, "balance" would slip away imperceptibly over time until I was left again with only the blackest pitch. I never realized the changes until I found myself back at the kitchen table, trying to figure out how to fix what wasn't working about my work. Trying to find my way out of the darkness again.

We all know that standard metaphor based in airplane safety, that we need to affix our own oxygen mask before helping others. And we try! Sometimes. Most of the time. Or we try really hard for a month, a week, a few days. But the work is so pressing; the needs are so great. We wonder: Is it even possible to fully and properly affix our own oxygen mask first? Or maybe we're one of those special people who can get by with a little less oxygen in general. (There are those people, right?) Maybe we tell ourselves everything is fine, even if the mask is only kind of half on, even if it's losing oxygen all around us, even if we're gasping like fish out of water.

When we don't get enough oxygen, we get a few warning signs, like a headache, to let us know something is amiss. Whether we notice it or not, our heart beats faster, working harder to try and get oxygen throughout our body. But if we don't address the issue, a headache quickly turns to confusion and even more dangerous effects.

The parallels to when work becomes all-consuming are clear. What started as mission-driven work has morphed into something we barely recognize. The warning signs may have been there, but just like with low oxygen, it's easy to overlook a headache and push on. Some of us even come to a crisis, a complete inability to keep going in the work, and we require drastic lifesaving measures. I've seen my friends in helping professions require medical leave from work due to physical or emotional burnout. I've seen friends neglect their health for years, grinding away, until a heart attack, stroke, or other significant diagnosis forces a change. But even still, for some of us, even after these drastic measures and recovery, we can find ourselves *right back* in the same low-oxygen environment as before. Maybe you've seen it. Maybe you've lived it.

This cycle is not inevitable. Having work that is of service to the world does not require a life of monastic self-sacrifice. And on some level, we know this, or at least we *want* to know it. This is why we continually search for the elusive "balance."

We're good at our work, and we're proud of it. We're proud that we can make a difference, that people can depend on us, that we have stories of lives changed due, at least in part, to our showing up day after day.

So I've written this book to tell you: There is nothing wrong with you. There is nothing wrong with finding great satisfaction and meaning in your work. If you've been struggling for your entire working life (maybe trying a few different jobs or even careers in the process) to find work-life balance, it's not your fault that you haven't found it. Because—hear me now—work-life balance is a lie.

I believed this lie myself for so long, but there's another way. And I've seen hundreds of others adopt this different way, this more *holistic* way, of thinking about our work and lives, too, finally freeing them from the endless treadmill of chasing "balance." This new perspective isn't *exactly* magical. (Though it can sometimes feel that way when the weight you've been carrying finally lifts!) It won't actually add more minutes to your day, make your boss more understanding, or make your family's needs less immediate. What it will do, though, is make sure that you are the boss of you. First, let's unpack why "balance" is not and has never been the answer, so we can finally stop chasing a fiction.

Work-Life Balance Is a Lie

Work-life balance simply doesn't exist. Possibly not for anyone, and *definitely* not for us. For us, "work" is not simply a trading of life hours for a paycheck. No, our work is bigger. It is how we make a difference in the world. Our work is an inextricable *part* of our lives, and this is a good thing: it is the place where our unique personality, skills, and experiences meet the needs of the world.

The first problem with the idea of "work-life balance" is that it implies that work and life are wholly separate constructs. I think of a balance scale with something called "life" on one side, and something called "work" on the other: two non-overlapping discrete elements. But to separate our work from our lives is impossible, because our work is an important part of our lives, and our lives are an important part of our work. Let me say that again: not only is our work an important part of our lives, *our lives* are also an important part of our work! We bring all of ourselves, all our experiences, talents, and dispositions to our work, too.

I think the circulatory system provides a helpful analogy for this idea. In our bodies, we have arterial blood and venous blood. Arterial blood flows through our arteries, pumped by the heart, and is bright red in color, full of oxygen. Venous blood flows through our veins and is a dark red color, though it looks blue or purple through translucent skin. It has less oxygen and is returning to the heart and lungs. The thing is, we don't just have arteries and veins. We have also the capillaries, the connectors between the arterial system and the venous system. Our capillaries are only two layers of cells thick, so small that our red blood cells have to pass through in single file. And we need them everywhere; it's estimated that the average human has about forty billion capillaries. In the capillaries, we can't really tell the arterial blood from the venous blood anymore. We know that the blood enters the capillary system as arterial blood and leaves as venous blood, but the in-between defies categorization. The capillaries are the liminal spaces, and they're where the magic happens, because it's in these tiny capillaries that our blood can serve our whole bodies. The capillaries are where our other tissues receive life-sustaining oxygen and nutrients, where our white blood cells can launch an attack against infection. It's where carbon dioxide and other waste products are picked up and carried away.

What if instead of viewing our work and our lives as non-overlapping discrete elements, like venous blood and arterial blood, we started viewing them as part of an interconnected system, just like our capillaries? What if we could find ways for our work and our nonwork to be in service to our whole lives, in the same way that the capillary system serves our whole bodies? And one more idea for your consideration: what if it is the *overlap* between our work and our nonwork, and the exchange between them, that is essential for our highest functioning?

The second issue with this "work-life balance" idea is that it implies that there is a correct proportion of "work" to balance "life." That there's a right answer, a set ratio, and when we find it, we'll magically feel the bliss of this thing called "balance."

Looking for "balance" reminds me of how food scientists have a "bliss point" that they work hard to find. They tinker and tinker, looking for the exact right amount of salt, fat, sweet, and crunch that will make a food irresistible. But here's the thing: your life is not a potato chip. There is no set point of "balance" that will provide ultimate bliss. We are whole people, living our whole lives. There just isn't a universal ratio that is true for all people, or even the same person across their whole lives. We all have seasons of our lives, various chapters, and our work will adapt and change as we do.

We can spend our working lives searching for this elusive "balance," but we won't find it. We can try all the tips and tricks (some of which have merit), but if we're doing the right things in pursuit of the wrong goal, we're not likely to get where we're going.

We know this when it comes to physical travel. If I want to take a pleasant road trip to Nashville from my home in Virginia, there are plenty of great things for me to do. Before I set off, I get my car tuned up and pack a cooler of healthy snacks. On the trip, I stop every couple of hours at beautiful or interesting places to walk and get some fresh air. I have music and podcasts and audiobooks queued up, and I keep the temperature inside the car just right. I've done all the right things to have a great trip. But if I'm doing these good things in pursuit of the wrong goal, by driving in the direction of New York instead of Nashville, I'm not going to feel bliss upon arrival. I'm going to feel frustrated that all my hard work and planning didn't pay off like it was "supposed to."

Maybe you've even been there, feeling misled or even angry about how your work and life seem to be in opposition to one another, that things are not at all as you planned. Many of us have wondered "Is this really what I signed up for?" And that's the danger of pursuing balance. Striving for an impossibility is only going to make us frustrated. Worse, burnout can soon follow. Burnout research indicates that a primary driver of clinical burnout is a mismatch between what we feel we should be able to do (i.e., meet our job demands) and our actual resources to meet those demands.

We want our work to be of service to the world. We want to support the full thriving of others.

But what can we do, then, if we're not thriving ourselves?

We have to shift our focus from balance to alignment.

Out of Balance, Into Alignment

noun: *alignment*

1 arrangement in a straight line, or in correct or appropriate relative positions.

2 a position of agreement or alliance.

I'll admit it, sometimes I skip over reading definitions like this in a book. (I mean, I know what words mean!) But look again. Both definitions of alignment are useful for our consideration. Take your time here. Seriously, read those two definitions again.

In the first definition, "alignment" can be used to show when two items are in "correct or appropriate relative positions." This is a physical definition. Wheels on a car need to be in alignment, tiles in a pattern have a particular alignment. And yet, I think it provides some utility when we think more metaphorically, considering how we might bring our work and our nonwork into "correct or appropriate relative positions" in our lives. I especially love that in this first definition we're considering how these positions are *relative*. They aren't fixed, like some idea of "balance." They might ebb and flow over time and with situations.

The best way, then, to think of our lives is not as a giant scale with work and life opposing one another. The best way to think of our lives is as a **mosaic**.

If you think of your life as an ever-expanding magical piece of mosaic art, alignment means you get to choose where each piece is placed. Maybe it's a piece worthy of a front-and-center location, or maybe it's a more peripheral piece for now. Maybe it's a bright hue to pop, or maybe it's a connector piece—still important, but not garnering great attention.

And as you choose, you can also evaluate whether the work pieces and nonwork pieces in your life are relative to each other in the way that best serves you right now. (And anyway, isn't that what people really mean when they say that they want more "balance" in their lives? That they don't want the work pieces they've picked up to crowd out their most precious and beautiful nonwork pieces?) We all want our work and our nonwork to be in the correct relative position to each other, whatever that looks like for us. Our mosaic is unique, utterly incomparable to someone else's.

But I think the positions of work and nonwork are relative in another way, too. (They're doubly relative!) This second relativity is due to the fact that the correct positions aren't fixed forever, that they can change over the course of our lives and with different circumstances. This is why our life mosaic is a bit magical. Over the course of our lives, we can arrange and rearrange our pieces; we can grow them and shrink them.

We can lose them for a time, and we can welcome them back. We can add new pieces, and we can shift where the center lies. We can also grow our mosaic altogether, creating even more space for the things we love (but we'll address those strategies in the second part of this book).

For now, it's probably obvious that our priorities shift over the course of our lives. An aligned life for a father with young children may have different relative positions for work pieces and nonwork pieces than his aligned life did before having children. Retirement will bring another realignment. In fact, life changes of all kinds, including health changes, family changes, and employment or career changes, are all likely to create shifts in the relative positions of our work pieces and nonwork pieces. Yet alignment is still possible at every stage of our life journeys. And since we will inevitably grow and change over the course of our lives, we want to learn to be attentive. As our lives evolve, the ideal positions for our work and nonwork can change for us, too. Our ever-shifting mosaic can be beautiful at every stage.

The second definition of alignment also provides a powerful way of thinking for us. Alignment can be used to indicate "a position of agreement or an alliance." Think about this for a second, an *alliance*. What if we stopped striving for some impossible, made-up construct called "balance" and instead started focusing on maintaining a healthy **alliance** among our many work and nonwork pieces?

Stay with me here. Countries make alliances, groups make alliances, and individuals make alliances. Every time, it is a show of mutual support. An alliance is all about a public commitment to having one another's back. When you make an alliance, you are "for" the other party. You can be counted on. You are agreeing to support, and to never undermine, their best interests.

Did you know that some mosaic artists, both ancient and modern, create their art without any glue? These mosaics hold together purely by the fit and strength of all the pieces, each supporting the others. That's a healthy alliance!

The beautiful mosaic of the Pantheon floor in Rome is often considered such an example. When I'm in Rome, I usually try to stay near the Pantheon. It's thrilling to see the enormous doors open and close, because each door weighs about 7.5 tons, and yet can be moved by just one or two people per door! My favorite thing about the Pantheon besides its beauty, though, is how it connects Rome through the ages. The structure itself is incredibly ancient, built in the early part of the second century. It has served many purposes over the years, from a Roman temple to a Christian church, a royal tomb, an architectural model (for St. Peter's Basilica, the US Capitol Building, and the Rotunda at my alma mater of the University of Virginia), and now a historical landmark (and church). It houses the tombs of Renaissance painter Raphael, along with Italian royalty like King Victor Emmanuel II, who was the first king of a unified Italy.

The Pantheon has stood for nearly two thousand years, with daily visitors numbering in the tens of thousands; millions of people every year. The famous oculus, open to the sky, means the rains of those nearly two thousand years have fallen on those floor tiles. And yet, scholars estimate that at least one third of the stones in the floor are still "original," meaning not restored in modern times. And while some mortar and grouting was likely used, the ancient artists and designers also created the floor so that the weight of each piece, coupled with support from the weight of the surrounding pieces, would be the primary means of holding the whole mosaic in place. Each piece supports the others, and the strength of this support has allowed the mosaic to endure.

What if our work and our nonwork pieces could be in alliance, too? What if the presence of each piece supporting the others is exactly how our whole life mosaic holds together?

We have a new opportunity: to be in alliance with *ourselves*. *We* are the ones who won't let us down. "We are the ones we have been waiting for," as poet June Jordan once wrote. And our work and our nonwork become *co-contributors* to a meaningful and satisfying life.

And isn't *that* the whole point? Why we chose our professions in the first place? To bring our whole selves in service to our missions? To have this meaningful and satisfying life? To know that our individual brand of magic, made up of our unique capabilities, temperaments, and experiences, can make a difference in the lives of others?

So, unlike the concept of "balance," a huge life scale where there's a correct amount of work weight on one side and a correct amount of life weight on the other to zero the scale, alignment doesn't ask us to split work and life 50–50, 60–40, or by any other ratio. Alignment offers us 100 percent. We can be whole people living our whole lives, with our work and nonwork in harmony and even supporting and enhancing one another.

Alignment leaves no room for burnout, because when you align your life mosaic by prioritizing the things that matter most to you, you come home to yourself. And the best part is, an aligned life is possible at every stage of your life journey. This book will provide you with the tools to recognize and make changes when your life is out of alignment, so that you can find joy and meaning in all parts of your life, for the rest of your life.

Introducing a Montessori Approach

I had my first glimpses of moving beyond work-life balance when I started my training to become a Montessori teacher. At the time, I was already five years into my teaching career, and I had already had "the talk" more than once.

Montessori teacher training is not a small commitment, and it would be easy to see it as just a huge weight on the "work" side of the work-life balance scale. Most teachers do, at least at the start. I was incredibly fortunate to be sponsored by my school for the tuition and travel, but the credential I was seeking still required over five hundred hours of class time, as well as a year-long teaching practicum. But I think the thing that made Montessori training the most daunting (and also the most impactful) was that I quickly realized I was not just learning a new way to teach, I was learning a new way to *be* in the world. That's no small task. Clearly, this training was going to be about more than just my "work."

In my first summer of training, I noticed that my mentors in the training program worked hard and took their work seriously, but they had a lightness and joy about their work as well. One instructor, Barb, shared a quote about "a master in the art of living" on the first day of our super-intense curriculum development course. Maybe you've heard it? It's often been misattributed, but Lawrence Pearsall Jacks wrote in 1932 that: "A master in the art of living draws no sharp distinction between his work and his play, his labour and his leisure, his mind and his body, his education and his recreation. He hardly knows which is which. He simply pursues his vision of excellence through whatever he is doing and leaves others to determine whether he is working or playing. To himself he always seems to be doing both."

Now, there have been plenty of critiques about this line of thinking; you've probably seen the sarcastic memes that tell you *not* to do what you love, because instead of living by the popular motivational quote, "Find a job you love, and you will never have to work a day in your life," you'll actually be "working every day of your life with no boundaries." Of course, boundaries are important, as we'll discuss in Chapter 7, but should we all go spend significant portions of our precious life on work that we hate? If we have no other options for making ends meet and taking care of our families, that's one thing. And if you're reading this book, it's likely that you already have a job that you find meaningful! So what I loved about the Jacks quote, and about what my Montessori mentors were showing me, was that there was a more holistic way to think about our work.

I had come from a hard-charging, high-achieving academic paradigm, where it was clear to me from an early age that there were winners and losers in the world. But my Montessori instructors were showing me a different possibility, one where every human could be seen as inherently worthy, with unique gifts to offer the world. Our job as educators, they were showing me, was not to view students as "empty vessels," waiting to be filled up with knowledge, but as uniquely capable, talented, and curious beings, who were already engaged in the important work of self-construction. Our job was to create the environment where each human could blossom into the fullest expression of *themselves*. And I quickly realized, with some shock, that this applied to *us* as adults, too! It was no longer about being the best *in* the world, it was about being the best *for* the world, as Dewitt Jones has said.

And Montessori education has had some impressive outcomes. To name just a few examples, educational researchers have found evidence that a Montessori education may be an effective intervention in narrowing educational achievement gaps, that the brains of Montessori students show evidence of embedding new knowledge in a more flexible way, fostering deeper learning and more knowledge transfer than non-Montessori students, and that adults who experienced a Montessori education reported significantly higher well-being scores than adults who experienced conventional education.

Montessori training absolutely taught me a lot about being an effective teacher, with lessons on learning and how the brain works, adolescent development, how to prepare a classroom, how to promote divergent and critical thinking, and more. But it also prioritized my own human development. We had lessons on effective communication and conflict resolution, on how to own our own stories, while being mindful that our viewpoint is just one, and often limited. We learned how to reframe our thinking and even our self-talk, to believe in the "not yet," and to reframe failures as growth opportunities, not evidence of *being* a global failure.

I've served as the director of this same Montessori teacher education program now for over a decade, and in that time, I've seen this Montessori approach transform literally hundreds of adults, not just their students.

And from my work as a Montessori teacher, teacher educator, scholar, and leader, it's become crystal clear to me that these lessons don't have to be reserved for the tiny percentage of humans who are able to receive a Montessori education (though I'm encouraged that Montessori education is growing worldwide, and especially in public schools) or the even tinier percentage of humans who receive formal Montessori teacher training. No, I think these lessons of embracing our fullest humanity can be for everyone. We can all learn to design and redesign our precious life mosaics, to find joy and meaning in all the parts of our lives, including our work!

I remember Ben, who came to our training and was a most enthusiastic student. However, when he decided to leave teaching, he wrote me the most heartwarming email, thanking the program for changing his life. He wrote about how his Montessori training had shown him that his deepest passion was actually for farming, for working on and with the land. And while his role as a Montessori teacher would allow him to dabble in that work, he felt that his life and his family would be best served if he dedicated himself to that work full-time.

I'll never forget Saundra, who shared that her Montessori training experience gave her the courage to fight for her marriage. Or Sofia, whose training experience gave her the courage to leave hers. (Her exact words: "solo time saved my life.")

I've even known adults who, upon studying Montessori for themselves, reported life-changing impacts. One friend of mine, Melissa, reported that learning about Montessori education gave her enough hope and confidence to bring a child into the world, after many years of being uncertain. Her daughter, now eight, is thriving in her Montessori school.

My trainers kept nudging us that if we were going to participate in a form of education that prioritizes the holistic development of healthy human beings, that we, too, could be included in that. *Our* healthy and holistic development also mattered! And as I've studied more on adult development, it's clear that Montessori concepts have applicability for the capacity-building of everyone.

My Vantage Point

I also want to take a moment to honor and recognize that I am writing from my own perspective, a place shaped by significant privilege. As an able-bodied, neurotypical, cisgender white American woman in a stable and loving heterosexual relationship, I recognize that my intersecting identities are not often marginalized in the society in which I live. I know that this is not equally true for everyone.

And yet, whoever we are, we are whole people. No matter our background or perspective, I still believe that alignment is for everyone, for all of us. I believe this because we are all whole humans, and we are all worthy of thriving. And so it is my hope that others will come along and expand these ideas, further developing a roadmap for what alignment looks like in individuals with different perspectives from mine. Because, while I believe that alignment is for everyone, we all experience different challenges on our journey, and we will need additional voices to contribute to this conversation.

If these ideas are calling to you, I hope that maybe you, dear reader, will be one of these contributing voices. Maybe you will be the one to share with others what alignment looks like in your life, and maybe you will become the inspiration for many more voices. Because I know that there are a lot of people out there who see in this problem a reflection of their own struggles. Of loving and feeling committed to their work in the world, but also struggling not to be consumed by it, and so striving over and over again for the elusive balance.

If you see yourself here, then this book is a labor of love from my heart to yours. I believe with all my heart that it *is* possible to thrive in work and in our messy, complicated, and beautiful lives, while still making a difference in the lives of others. We'll walk this journey of alignment and realignment together, and we'll look at specific aspects of our lives that have special potential to increase or decrease our thriving. And at the end of this book, you'll know how to recognize and make changes when work isn't working. We only have one tiny and treasured life. We want our whole lives, every part of us, to thrive, and to contribute to the greater thriving of others.

I'm so glad you picked up this book and that you've allowed me to walk this path with you. I write as someone only a little further down the road. I certainly don't have it all figured out. But this is the book I wish I had had in my early days of teaching, where everything was always too much and never enough. It's the book I wrote for my sister caring for her oncology patients, who would come home after fifteen hours of work and cry in the kitchen. It's the book I wrote for the young lawyer in legal aid, the community organizer, the social worker. And it's the book I wrote for you, in hopes you will find greater alignment and thriving in your one tiny and treasured life.

A Montessori Model of a Book

Montessori classrooms try to offer as much choice as possible to students, and since I will always be a teacher at heart (although sometimes we Montessorians will also call ourselves "guides") I wanted to share some choices for your reading approach, too.

The first section of the book, Reframing Our Relationship with Work, is designed to be read in order, with each chapter's ideas building upon the prior material and setting the stage for the second part of the book. Then the second section of the book, Supporting a Healthy Alliance, has chapters that can be read in any order, but which won't make much sense without the first five chapters under your belt. So you might choose to read this book straight through (as I usually do for books like this) or you might choose to follow the first five chapters with whatever feels most urgent or helpful right now, such as Chapter 8, if you're navigating some life changes and eager to apply alignment principles to your current experiences.

In addition, this book has a variety of exercises, practice opportunities, and reflection questions. And all I can offer you here is my best teaching advice: the more students practice with and think about the material at hand, the more internalized it will become. This is simply how learning works! It's our brain wiring: neural connections in our brains are strengthened through repeated use. Practice with a new concept makes recall and application possible, then even prompt and painless. (I won't claim "perfect.")

In the Montessori training program, we often remind teachers that "telling isn't teaching," meaning just because something was said, doesn't mean it was learned. And one of the more fascinating ideas (to me, anyway) embedded in Montessori teaching and learning is the concept of the three-period lesson. Basically, a three-period lesson has (as you might guess) three parts to the teaching and learning.

The first period, as we like to explain it, is the "gift" of information. It's the introduction to a concept. The second period is the practice, and the third period is the assessment, the application of the new learning. It's simple, but most of my secondary education didn't provide me with a lot of second period practice; it was more common to go from the first period lesson (usually a lecture) to a third period assessment (usually a test or quiz). But we were skipping the part where the neural connections of learning really happen. This is in the practice, where students interact with the material in different ways. Learning happens when our brains are actively engaged. Similarly for you, dear reader, simply reading about an idea or approach isn't likely to be the same as mastering it. And this is the tricky part, because our brains can convince us that we have internalized something when we recognize it, when it feels familiar, but that's not actually the same as deeply understanding something. A quick read-through of a new concept isn't usually enough to spark mastery. (Though *how* you read matters, because strategies like pausing to think about and consider the new ideas, journaling about them, explaining or debating them with others, and/or making annotations or notes for yourself to revisit later are all strategies that help the content to stick... again, because they all involve more interaction with the material and can serve as their own forms of second period practice.)

And so, if the narrative sections of each chapter are the "first period," I wanted to also offer you some choices in second period practice, where you could interact with the ideas to reinforce and better internalize them. These second period practice opportunities will come at the end of Chapters 1 through 8, and you might be a person who tries all of them or just a few here and there. I do hope you will give at least a few of them a try (I highly recommend that you try the writing activities!), to see what a difference it can make for internalizing the content. Plus, if you're reading this book with a friend, family member, partner, colleague, or book group, the second period practice opportunities might serve as activities you can try together, a place where you can support each other, or just a source to spark some rich discussions. Second period practice is practice. It's low stakes; it's not an assessment. I hope it might even feel playful at times. Feel free to journal or to discuss the reflection questions, which allow you to think about and engage with the content on a deeper level, before moving on to applying it. Reflection questions are the type of practice I've provided here, due to the nature of this book's content, but just in case you're a teacher looking to implement more second period practice in your own teaching, please remember that there are many other approaches to providing helpful practice opportunities. Students will need more than reflection questions to practice their learning on cellular respiration, for example.

The third period part of each lesson, the application of the new knowledge, is where you make the real changes in your life. It's where the learning has been fully internalized, so that you're able to apply it to your own context, your own life. It's also where you could teach it to someone else; peer teaching and learning is a beautiful part of the Montessori classroom, too. So I'll have some suggestions for third period applications, too, but just like there are infinite ways to practice with new learning, you don't need to be limited by my suggestions. Applying new knowledge to your life can take many forms, and *you* are the ultimate authority on which applications are most needed in your life.

A book can change your life, but only if you engage with it. And you're here now. You know that your work matters, and I hope you know also that *you* matter more. So if you've come to this book, dear reader, to learn more about how to craft your life mosaic so that you can find full thriving in all parts of your life, for the rest of your life, I hope you'll take as much time as you need here. (We're only talking about *your whole life!*)

And good news! You don't have to wait another minute to start moving into alignment.

CHAPTER 1 SECOND PERIOD: THE PRACTICE

Writing Activity

Write down 10 to 20 important pieces of your life mosaic, whatever comes to mind for you first. You can list them or draw them like mosaic pieces. (If you draw them, feel free to make them different sizes, as you see fit!)

Don't be afraid to be specific. For example, if you have a child who plays soccer, and it's important to you to attend as many games as possible for this season of their (and your) life, "soccer games" might be one of your mosaic pieces. That's much more specific than listing simply "family," because the family pieces of your life are many! Likewise, you might list your work projects or responsibilities as separate pieces. They're all a part of your work, but you probably value the different pieces in different ways.

Reflection Questions

- Once you have your list (from the writing activity above) does anything stand out to you about what came to mind first? Do you feel like this list is a reflection of your current priorities? Or what feels pressing right now? Or is it something else entirely?

- On a scale of 1 to 10, how strong is the alliance among your work pieces and your nonwork pieces right now? How well does each piece support your overall thriving?

- While the number of mosaic pieces that can make up our lives is nearly infinite, look back at the pieces you listed (in the writing activity above). Which mosaic pieces need more time and attention right now, and which pieces would you like to shrink a little?

- If you could instantly make more space in your life mosaic, what pieces would you like to add? Are there any you could safely remove?

CHAPTER 1 THIRD PERIOD: THE APPLICATION

Take the First Step

If you've had "the talk," are worried that you *might* have "the talk," or if you feel like your most important people have *wanted* to give you "the talk," there's something you can do right now to make a difference. This book is going to help you see how shifting from a pursuit of "balance" to "alignment" changes everything about how we view our work and lives. With the alignment model, you will have a framework for making decisions about all the important pieces of your life's mosaic, so that when conflicts inevitably arise, you have a way of making decisions about unexpected demands on your time and attention. But it will take time to learn and internalize all these ideas, and then some more time to practice them.

But I don't believe that we do hard things alone. So my invitation to you right now is to take a first step towards alignment, even before we've fully covered the alignment process. To do this, think about your most important people, the people who have maybe given you "the talk," or wanted to. We're going to bring them in on the idea that you've started this journey towards alignment, to consider all the important work and non-work pieces of your life.

So right now, choose your plan. Are you going to share face-to-face? Write an email? Send a text? Handwrite a love letter?

There are likely two pieces of communication that need to be exchanged. First, your person needs to know that you see them. If they've raised concerns, let them know that you hear them. They need to know that you now fully recognize the problem, that you have not been able to find the (imaginary) work-life balance you have been seeking. Let them know that you are now taking the first steps in figuring out how to keep your important work from crowding out the precious nonwork parts of your life, because you are reading this book. Ask for their patience and support as you start this journey towards alignment, and let them know that you'd like to stay in conversation about these ideas and your progress.

Second, if your person feels differently about their work than you do about yours, they may not fully understand how or why your work matters to you so much. If you suspect that this may be part of the problem, the second part of your conversation or email can also be to invite them into your work. Help them see why your work matters so much to you. You might consider sharing from one or more of the following prompts:

- I chose this profession because…
- On my best days, I know I make a difference because…
- People depend on me for…
- If I am not able to do my work well, I feel…
- When I am not at work, I still enjoy thinking about…
- I am proud of my work because…

I'm betting that your person loves you and wants to support you. So take the first step, and let them share this journey of alignment with you.

2

Let's Face It, Our Work Is Personal (And That's Okay!)

AFTER FIVE DAYS of being on a working farm with twenty-something middle school students, sleeping in tents, and ensuring that all students were safe and fed (while still learning!) I staggered through the front door. I dropped my bags, peeling the clothing off as I went, and headed straight to the shower, my first since leaving.

"How did it go?" Jonathan called.

"Good," came my monosyllabic answer. I was now mimicking the thirteen-year-old students with whom I had spent the week.

The trip had been an incredible success, but it was always bittersweet. Field studies were among the most demanding but also the most rewarding parts of my job as a Montessori teacher. They were a chance to teach students the kinds of lessons that simply aren't possible within the four walls of our classroom. This year had offered the chance for us to engage in three multi-day field studies, for a total of twelve days and one weekend away. It was joyful work, but it is also a sacrifice for both teachers and their families to navigate this time away. And while I have always truly loved working with adolescents, it still takes tremendous energy, patience, and good humor to wrangle large numbers of middle school students 24-7, while making sure all the necessary logistics fall into place over nearly a week. It's a labor of love to be sure.

And the spring trip especially had a special place in my heart. It was a chance to celebrate community, engage on a deeper level, and bear witness to an important rite of passage. For my students, they were doing the most important work of becoming. They are keenly aware of leaving childhood behind and of considering who they are and who they will be as they prepare for high school and beyond.

But I'll also be honest that camping has never been my favorite activity. It's good for me to do hard things every once in a while, and I have yet to see anything that comes close to multi-day camping trips for supporting healthy adolescent development. So while I appreciate that some outdoorspeople love the snug feeling of being in a sleeping bag in the great outdoors, I am not such a person. No, while I adore my nature walks and time outside, I will always prefer a warm, dry bed inside where there are no insects to bite me. But sleep is always a luxury on these trips for the supervising adults, because one is always half listening for the unzipping of tents, trying to make sure everyone stays safely tucked in for the night.

It wasn't uncommon for me to return from such an experience with the start of a head cold, and this time was no exception. I could feel it coming on as I let the heat and steam of the shower wash away the farm grime and bring some relief to my sinuses. I wasn't surprised at the tickle in my throat: in addition to the physical exhaustion, there were some important emotions. In other years this spring trip had been about holding space, a liminal experience for my students who were preparing for their next stage: the eighth graders heading off to various high schools in the area, and the seventh graders saying goodbye to their eighth-grade friends and preparing to take over the leadership roles of the middle school. But this year, I was in my own in-between space. I had made the difficult decision that it was time for me to take on a new role as teacher educator, while at the same time starting my doctoral studies. My own identity was shifting right along with my students', and it was the usual mix of excitement and terror.

After my shower, I poured myself a drink and melted into the couch, waiting for the dinner takeout I had ordered. I should have left my work email closed, as it had been all week, but old habits die hard. Maybe I wanted to see if anything interesting had happened at school while we were off the grid. Maybe I wondered if there were any notes of thanks or updates from a student or parent. But when I clicked open a particular email that had landed in my inbox while I was away, I had to read it three times *and* practice my breathing.

In addition to the usual junk mail and notices, there was one important-looking email from a member of our school's administrative team. The note was simple and straightforward. Businesslike. I was informed that with absences due to the death of my grandmother and the flu I caught earlier that school year, plus two planned personal days, I was over my allotted days off, and my last month's paycheck would be reduced accordingly.

My mind raced, and I was feeling more than a little slighted. It didn't seem to matter that I had gone above and beyond my contractual obligations with not one or even two, but three overnight field studies with students that year, including an entire weekend away. Or that for any absence, and even in the midst of my flu, I had made sure lessons plans were available and emailed daily, so that my colleagues (usually not a paid sub) had what they needed to minimize the disruption and burden, and I continued grading at home. Or that I was pretty sure bereavement leave wasn't supposed to count against our time off.

Now, to be clear, this email wasn't sent with any ill will or malice. The administrator sending the email was doing as requested, following procedures. It probably wasn't meant to be a reflection on how valuable I was as a teacher or member of the school community.

But in the moment, I felt like I had been punched in the gut. Like all my work—not just this year, but over my time at this institution—was being devalued. I couldn't escape feeling that perhaps all the times I had gone above and beyond in my work only made me a pushover, because all that mattered in the end was the contractual obligations, the letter of the law. That was what the email was showing me. And maybe I would have been more prepared for such an email if I had been working a nine-to-five job for a huge corporation, I don't know. But somehow, it seemed to hurt more coming from the Montessori school, especially on the heels of our spring trip.

When I went in the next Monday to discuss, I was calm, but my feelings hadn't changed much. The administrator I spoke with seemed pretty shocked to hear my perspective. To appease me, she insisted "Katie, this isn't personal." But what I struggled to explain was that this matter was nothing if not personal to me. In that moment, the conversation was all about my work; in fact, it was a straight-up valuation of my work *in dollars*, and my work has always been personal.

I was reminded of Julia Roberts's powerful portrayal of Erin Brockovich in the movie of the same name. If you're not familiar with *Erin Brockovich*, it's an incredible story of a woman who takes a job with a small legal office to pay the bills. She hadn't had a lot of formal higher education; she's a single mom juggling a million personal things, and she's really meant to be someone who only takes care of some paperwork. But her paperwork leads her to a startling discovery: tons of people, mostly folks of limited means and education, have been falling sick. Babies, children, pregnant women, you name it. And Erin realizes that it's because of the water. Not only that, she realizes that the water company *knew* there was an issue and that they covered it up. Erin goes door-to-door to engage with the people, hearing their concerns and winning their trust, in order to build the case they require to get those people the financial compensation they need and deserve.

She shows grit and perseverance, determination and ingenuity, all while finding some creative solutions to her own family's needs. When her boss haphazardly comments that she shouldn't get angry (and how often have we seen others patronize strong feelings, and especially the anger of women?) by saying "You're emotional, you're erratic. You say anything... you make this personal, and it isn't." Erin responded with lines I've never forgotten: "NOT PERSONAL?!? That is my WORK, my SWEAT, and MY TIME AWAY FROM MY KIDS! IF THAT IS NOT PERSONAL, I DON'T KNOW WHAT IS!"

Julia Roberts stirred my soul with the delivery of those lines.

Our Work Is Personal (And That's Okay!)

If you're reading this book, I bet you know something about personal work. When you wake up thinking about other people's children, when you grieve the loss of a patient, when you dream about the people you serve, working to promote the full human thriving of others, your work *is* personal. And any suggestion to the contrary can feel like a slap in the face.

There's lots of advice out there, though, that personalizing your work is a bad idea. That the workplace, the boss, the company will take every ounce that you're willing to give and then still want more before they use you up and spit you out. We're told that work shouldn't be our identity, that we shouldn't prioritize work over our "real" lives, and anyone who gives "too much" (an unknowable, indefinable amount, but never mind) must be a workaholic. And because lies have the best chance of being believed when they contain a kernel of truth, it's unfortunately not hard to find some good reasons for these warnings to exist. But they lack nuance. They're not true in all situations or for all people. And they might not be true for you. Because there is nothing inherently wrong with caring about your work, with having your work as an important priority in your life. Your time may be finite, but your self, your you-ness, your essence is infinite. That means that giving of yourself doesn't have a limit. *You* are a renewable resource.

And, since our beliefs shape our reality, let's unpack the problems with the messages that tell us otherwise.

I have two primary problems with the kind of advice that runs along the lines of "never forget your real life isn't at work." First, these notions still promote the false idea of "balance," implying that there can be a clear division between our work and our "real" lives. But we are whole humans, with one life mosaic. What happens at our workplace impacts our life outside of the workplace, and vice versa, because our mosaic pieces are connected to each other. When I've had a truly great day at work, everything else in my life seems a little brighter too. I've had days where I've had as much fun teaching students as I have had on the best days of vacation. Teaching and traveling are *both* important parts of my life mosaic. They're not opposites trying to "balance" one another.

The TV show *Severance* explores these exact themes in a powerful way. Billed as a psychological thriller, *Severance* focuses on a fictional workplace, where employees undergo a surgical procedure that divides their memories between the workplace and their life outside of the office building. When they get on the elevator to arrive at work each day, workers lose all memory of their life outside work. Similarly, when they get on the elevator to leave work, they lose all memory of what happened at work. *Severance* premiered in early 2022, shortly after all the work-life "balance" conversations that happened during the COVID-19 shutdowns. We see that the main character, wracked with grief from losing his wife, chooses the procedure so that he can find relief from missing his wife and be functional at work. But the show functions as a kind of dire warning about the goal of compartmentalizing our lives. It shows, in pretty stark terms sometimes, that a divide between work and life, if played out to a logical conclusion, is dehumanizing. The characters are not allowed access to their full selves.

The second problem that I have with these societal warnings that work must be separated from our "real lives" is that they don't take into account the kind of work that is happening. They don't consider meaningful work. And there's solid evidence that work can be a great source of meaning and satisfaction. Numerous studies have confirmed that feeling like your work matters is one of the greatest predictors of human thriving. Similarly, but on the other side, studies have shown that jobs that *don't* hold any meaning for people, explored in works like *Bullshit Jobs* by David Graeber, can have a negative impact on our well-being. (And may well be a place where a person chooses to limit themselves.) Research has even shown that thriving at work is positively correlated with thriving in nonwork spheres of life; researchers could find "no evidence" that thriving at work had negative impacts on a person's thriving levels outside of work. But the point is, having work that matters to you and making that work a priority in your life doesn't make you naïve; it makes your life richer!

As a teacher, I sometimes entertained the thought experiment of what would happen if I only worked my contractual obligations, and not a second more. (Usually this happened when I reviewed my contract listing my ordinary work obligations as 8:00 a.m. to 3:30 p.m., for a total of 37.5 hours per week. Also, at the time of this writing, salaried teachers in the United States, including adjunct instructors for universities, are not eligible for overtime pay, nor are they subject to minimum wage protections.) And while I got much more efficient in my work as I gained experience, I didn't see how I could possibly do my work in a way that made me happy and proud if I only worked those hours, turning myself into a kind of teacher bean counter. I *knew* the joy I could often find in the work. I loved reading students' notes and emails to me, planning interesting lessons and activities, looking over assessments to see who needed what next, and feeling like I was part of a team with my colleagues, doing work that mattered. That said, because our time is finite, and teaching elements are not the only important pieces in our life mosaic, I'll *also* be the first to advocate for some reasonable expectations of and protections for teachers: limits to the number of students served, protected time in the workday for lesson planning and assessment review, adequate compensation, and more.

And I want to be clear here too, that exploitative work is never okay, and unfortunately, there's too much of this going on. Hospitals that chronically understaff are not okay; it's dangerous for patients (well documented) and harmful to the well-being of hospital staff (also well documented). It's simply not okay to draw on the compassion of caring professionals (who will usually do what they can to meet the needs of a patient, no matter how short-staffed the unit is) as a substitute for adequate staffing procedures. These are big, systemic issues, and I think these systemic failures are the reason we've seen some of the more reactionary approaches, such as "quiet quitting" (where workers do the bare minimum that is required of them in their jobs) or even the "lying flat" phenomenon. ("Lying flat" originated in China as a rebuttal to the intense work and achievement culture there, emphasizing a simple lifestyle with perhaps lower-paying, lower-stress jobs, or even a withdrawal from the workforce completely.)

But the fact was, by the time I felt established in my teaching career, I knew I would always work at least a few hours beyond my contractual obligations, and most of the time, I didn't resent it. Most of the time, it didn't even feel like work—at least not in the way we usually think of it.

Work Has a PR Problem

I became a Montessori teacher after five years of full-time teaching, but I had held various employment gigs for years before I became a teacher. I had worked in restaurants, in childcare settings, in youth development, and in labs. But learning about Montessori classrooms, and their unique perspective on work, changed my views about work forever. It was through this that I've come to believe that even the word "work," in our current culture, has a PR problem. Have you ever heard, "It's not supposed to be fun; that's why we call it work!" Or "it's called a job, not a vacation." These ideas indicate work must be synonymous with drudgery, that it is an inherently unpleasant and burdensome undertaking, one that no one would choose freely if they didn't have to. But Montessori classrooms don't see work that way at all.

My friend Heather shared a story with me about one of her students, named Max. Max was new to the Montessori school, but he seemed to be adjusting well, so Heather was surprised when Max's dad asked for a meeting, indicating that something was amiss.

Max's dad shared with Heather that while it was great that Max seemed to like his Montessori school, the family was seeing big problems outside of school. He thought it might be about routines, that perhaps Max was simply having trouble adjusting to the weekend days that were less routine. He told Heather, "You see, Max cries most weekend mornings. And not even after anything has actually happened! He just seems to wake up and burst into tears!" Max's dad was perplexed. He loved weekends, and he wanted his family to revel in their time together, not start the day with a meltdown.

In the course of the conversation, Max's dad shared that he had the habit of waking up and joyfully announcing weekends by cheering to his family, "Hooray, hooray, no work today!"

"Ah," Heather told him, "that's it."

Max's dad gave her a look, the kind that said he definitely did not follow, and was also now somewhat suspicious about her sanity. "What's it?" he asked.

"The no work part," she said. "Here, in our Montessori classroom, all the interesting and engaging activities are called 'work,' not play. So to Max, an announcement of 'no work' might as well have been a proclamation of 'no fun today' first thing in the morning!"

Once this differing viewpoint of what "work" is became clear, Max's dad changed his weekend announcements, and Max didn't cry on weekends anymore. Because, perhaps unlike his dad, Max didn't see work as drudgery, or as a necessary evil. To Max, work was interesting, challenging, and in the challenge, even fun!

And after I had shared Max's story a few times, I started hearing more stories just like his. From Montessori teachers to Montessori parents, a theme of Montessori students feeling sad when they couldn't go to school turned out to be incredibly common. And I think that's because Montessori classrooms, with all their "work," are also containers for what might be the most important work of all: construction of the self.

When I speak with artists, writers, and other creatives, they understand these ideas that Montessori classrooms teach us about work and life. That our work is a part of our essence, and our creations, our work, are a part of both expressing and constructing ourselves.

Reframing what *work* means changes everything. It debunks the idea that work is onerous and allows us to reclaim joy and meaning both in and outside our places of employment. Because the truth is, our work is so much broader than we realize. And I don't believe you have to have been a Montessori student yourself to adopt a Montessori perspective of work.

Ten Things Montessori Classrooms Know About Work

As Max's story shows, Montessori schools, based on the ideas and research of Dr. Maria Montessori, have a particular view of work. In classrooms for very young children, there are specialized materials, which the children call "works." Indeed, all morning, students choose different activities and do their "work." In other early childhood classrooms, learning materials might be called "toys" and the work students do is called "play." But as any early childhood educator will tell you, play *is* a child's work. It's how they're figuring out the world around them, and their place within it.

While some find it strange that these young children "work" instead of "play" in their Montessori classrooms, I think that's often because we're bringing our own baggage to the terms. When you see these young people, so focused, so intent, so satisfied by their work, and then hear them recount with pride the work they did, I think it's aptly named. The term "work" gives weight to their activities. It marks them as important. A child who is working is not to be interrupted, not even by the teacher, unless absolutely necessary. Montessori programs go to great lengths to preserve extended blocks of time for students to find flow in their work. Work is a source of both pride and joy. And why shouldn't a young person's work be honored this way? In fact, what would society look like if we honored the work of everyone in this way? And besides that, if you have work that matters to you, you've probably also had moments where your work can overlap with your play.

When I became a Montessori teacher, I was inspired to find an educational philosophy dedicated to helping unlock the fullest potential of all humans. But I didn't grow up with a Montessori educational experience. And so, there were a few things for me to unlearn when I came to embrace a Montessori perspective. Things that I had considered unquestionably true, like the value of competition, needed reexamining (more on that point later). "Work" was another term that needed reassessment. To understand Montessori's approach to work, I had to unlearn some of the negative associations I had about work in order to not pass them along to students. The biggest connotation I had to unlearn was the idea that *work* was the opposite of *play* or *fun*.

Max already knew this, and he was only three!

So I got curious about what else I might be missing. Turns out, it was a lot! And I didn't fully absorb all these ideas in my training. It took time and practice, my work with Montessori students and teachers, my observations of and conversations with folks who have spent decades, if not lifetimes, working on behalf of children and adolescents. But as I grew in my understanding, I became convinced that these Montessori ideas were not just for young children or adolescents. Through my research and my work with adults, it was clear that there were important lessons from Montessori that could impact adult development, too.

But what was most amazing to me was that, over time, I found in these Montessori ideas a way to reframe my perspective of work. This reframe changed everything; it gave me space and permission to love my work *without* feeling that I was in danger of losing myself to it. It took me off the hamster wheel, chasing the false promise of "balance." And it helped me develop a new model for my life: a holistic mosaic that I can align and realign.

So to start, here are ten ideas from Dr. Maria Montessori, and the classrooms that bear her name, that can help us reframe our ideas about work. Each of these could probably be a book in and of themselves, but I'll share the shortest versions here.

1. Work is integral to and natural for humans; it is something that everyone does. Throughout history, humans have had a drive to create, connect, discover, explore, build, and share.

2. Work takes many forms and is not limited to economic exchange. Instead, work is simply our human endeavors, evidence of our life force. Our work is composed of our contributions to and our impact on the world.

3. Work is how we construct ourselves; it is an important part of our human development. I learned this first from my Montessori studies and observations of children and adolescents, but I've come to believe that it's true throughout our lives. Work can be a place where we build our sense of self, our positive self-regard, and our beliefs in our own capabilities and worthiness. Even as we get older, taking on new kinds of work (inside or outside the actual workforce) leads to continued self-construction and adult development.

4. Work is inherently noble, so we respect our own work and the work of others. Again, this comes back to the idea that work is evidence of our human capacity, vitality, and life

force. If all humans are inherently worthy of dignity and respect (a core Montessori belief), then so is their work. Very young students take great care to walk around peers who are working on the floor, because we would never want to inadvertently step on, interrupt, or undo part of someone's important work!

5. Since work has no negative connotations in a Montessori classroom, it can be a source of great joy and delight. In fact, in a Montessori classroom, there may be very little difference in how a child feels between engaging in something they call work (with a material) or in unstructured play. Now *that's* a lesson I was happy to learn!

6. Work can be self-satisfying; it doesn't require external approval to feel worthwhile. This is similar to the point on joy above, but I think it's worth mentioning explicitly. It seems obvious that of course we don't need someone else's approval to feel joy and meaning in our lives. But many of us have absorbed ideas from school and our places of employment that our work is only as good as the external validation it receives. Montessori schools aim to help students hone their own internal sense of possibility; to be the first responder to and assessor of their own work. The youngest students simply work on something until they feel internally satisfied, whether that's ten minutes, an hour, or several days. Older students have deadlines but constantly reflect on their work and progress.

7. Failure in our work is how we learn. Work is not meant to be completed perfectly while we're learning, so Montessori materials build in a "control of error," or a way for students to know on their own whether the desired

outcome was reached. If the material still shows an error, Montessori students simply start again. I've seen Montessori students work with a single material for an incredible amount of time, uninterrupted, until they feel internally satisfied. And even if it takes a long time, these students don't internalize any feelings of guilt, shame, or unworthiness at their mistakes. Mistakes are a normal part of the process, they are planned for in advance, and there are tools to help students self-correct.

8. Our environment (the container in which we do our work) has a huge impact on our ability to do work well. This also includes the human community where we work, because we work both independently and interdependently. So Montessori classrooms are highly structured and beautiful, with plants, natural light, and natural materials (usually not plastic), which promotes a sense of calm and order, so that students feel safe and free to focus. They provide students with furniture of the appropriate size for their bodies, adequate and flexible spaces for their work, learning materials that are accessible and complete, and clear classroom norms to help students understand how to respect the working environment for the benefit of everyone.

9. Focused work is important to prioritize, but it also has its limits, which leaves space for other experiences to promote holistic development. Montessori schools protect uninterrupted blocks of student work time, but they don't span the whole academic day. Typically, a Montessori work cycle (for early childhood and elementary levels) is three hours, leaving space for outdoor time, art and music, physical education, drama, going out, and other enrichment activities.

10 And finally, the most complex idea, Montessori believed that, as children grow to adulthood, work becomes a place where our unique brand of magic can meet the needs of the world. It engages the whole person and connects us with everything else in the universe, because we all have a role to play in contributing to the greater good.

You see, part of Montessori's idea for education was that it would be very broad, "cosmic" even. Montessori scholar and trainer Camillo Grazzini wrote about cosmic education by offering a metaphor, that we might think of the whole universe "as a great household, a cosmic household, where all the jobs involved in running the household have been divided up and shared." He went on to explain that Montessori's cosmic plan means that all beings "have tasks to fulfill, their cosmic work to accomplish."

Montessori believed that to teach things in isolation brings confusion, and so we need to see the whole, then the parts, then the whole again. Looking at our lives and our work as discrete and separate elements isn't in line with a cosmic perspective, where all things are interrelated, and where each of us has a unique purpose and role to fill in the universe.

Building on the ten lessons above, adopting a Montessori perspective of work in our lives would mean that, first, our work is important and should feel meaningful. This doesn't mean that every moment of our day is going to feel like we are saving the world. But we should be able to point to a bigger "why" for most of the work that we do.

Second, our work is to be respected. That means we don't disrespect earnest efforts of others or allow others to disrespect our work. It doesn't mean we can't benefit from feedback, self-evaluations, or other efforts towards continuous improvement. But we appreciate work product as evidence of the life energy of ourselves and others.

Third, our work connects us to others and to all of the universe. As we make a difference in our corner of the world, we can never know where the ripple effects will lead. I always connect this cosmic approach with the butterfly effect, from chaos theory, which says even seemingly small changes can have a massive impact in complex systems. The metaphor is that a butterfly flapping its wings might cause a tornado (or hurricane) on the other side of the world. I love thinking about being this butterfly... that we can never know where our influence will end, or even if it does. To me, it speaks of becoming infinite, that our essence can live on in the impacts we make.

Fourth, to find growth and meaning, work will have a "just right" challenge level and significant amounts of joy. We have to regularly step ourselves just outside of our safe zones—the pieces of work that we already know how to do well—and take on additional challenges. However, we shouldn't live in the panic zone, either. And while some days will always be better than others, if your commute to work brings nothing but dread on a daily basis, if you never have positive stories to celebrate about your work, something needs to change!

Fifth, work engages the whole person: we can bring all of who we are intellectually, emotionally, spiritually, socially, and even physically (as humans with bodies). This means our work will engage our head, hands, and heart, and that we can engage in our work with all parts of our identities, not feeling a need to hide essential parts of ourselves. It also means that we have a responsibility to spend time with who we are, as well as with what we do. Honing our craft at work cannot be separated from personal development. I've never forgotten the advice, widely attributed to author and speaker Jim Rohn, that, "your level of success will seldom exceed your level of personal development."

Our Paycheck Work and Our Purpose Work

Look, you're reading this book because you love your work, and you know that your work matters, but you don't want to feel that you've completely lost yourself to your work. You need a way to integrate the work that you love with the bigger picture, with all of who you are, so that the nonwork parts of your life can also shine. You may also need to gain clarity about what exactly your work *is*.

To write this book, I met via Zoom with an incredible and talented group of authors, each of us cheering one another on to show up and do the work necessary to share our messages with the world, to make a difference in the lives of our readers. One alumnus of the group shared a particular piece of wisdom about writing. He told another author who was struggling to wrangle a complicated idea to find the right story and clarify the point for her reader, that she didn't need to worry. That in fact, when you're writing a book, you're always writing your book, because whether you're physically involved in the act of writing or not, your mind and your subconscious are still activated, thinking things through, noticing new parallels. It's been true for me.

And this wasn't just true in my writing, it has been true in my teaching career as well. Sometimes, inspiration for a lesson, a new explanation for a complicated idea, or a new support to offer a student (adolescent *or* adult) would strike at the strangest times: when I was watching a movie, taking a walk, doing the dishes, or having coffee with a friend. Was

I "working" when these moments of inspiration struck? Well, yes and no! I was living my life—my full life, with all the joyful and mundane pieces of it. And because I am one whole human, with one brain, I can't automatically stop or turn off the "work" side of things. And most of the time, I wouldn't want to. When work is a joyful and meaning-giving part of my life, it can be a pleasure to have these moments of inspiration or connection. Maybe you've felt them, too: a joke you can't wait to share with a client or patient, a new idea to share that just might move your team forward in a problem you've been considering, or a story that helps illustrate and get colleagues on board with your mission.

If you're reading this book, your work is likely both your primary way of earning a living *and* at least part of the way you hope to show up and make a difference in the world. Yet these two things don't have to go together. There are plenty of people whose main income source is not also a primary source of meaning in their lives. And they're not all rich or retired, though financially independent people do have a particular life circumstance that can allow for this separation. What I've learned from speaking with such folks is that compensation simply has no bearing on how they value their work, or what they even consider their work to be. My instructor from Montessori teacher training, Barb (now a good friend), could be this way. After several decades of teaching, Barb scaled back but stayed employed as a teacher educator. One thing that amazed me (and if I'm honest, even frustrated me once or twice) was that Barb would often lose track of which work she was doing that was paid and which work she was doing that was volunteer. All of it was her work! All of it served the mission of her life. She was one whole human.

What if we thought of our work in this kind of holistic way? What if our work wasn't so much about the trading of life hours for compensation but was about our broader missions to the world? Now certainly our compensation matters, and everyone should be paid appropriately for the work that they do. But what if we took a cosmic approach?

So now that we've considered a broader definition of work, let's define some terms so that we can keep ourselves straight.

"Purpose work" is the term I'd like to use for this expanded vision, sometimes thought of as a calling or vocation. Your purpose work is what you are here now to be doing with your one tiny and treasured life, what Montessori folks might call your "cosmic task." Our purpose work can absolutely include paid employment, but it also includes meaningful activities done in taking care of family, friends, neighbors, and community. Advocacy, service, raising children, even voting—all these things can be a part of our purpose work. They all add a richness to our lives and make a difference in the world.

"Paycheck work" is the term I'd like to use for paid employment when the distinction is critical. If you're reading this book, it's likely that this is a large and important part of your purpose work. So while it's useful to have a term that specifically captures work related to our paid employment, most of the time this *is* what people mean by "work," and I use the simpler term often as well.

Many of us chose our occupations because we had a sense that this kind of work would indeed be at least part of the way that we make our world a better place. I'm simply suggesting that we don't have to be limited by the tasks and activities that pay us when we define our work. When we take this broader view, we see that our purpose work may include our methods of earning an income, but that it doesn't have to. And there is freedom in this realization. Because if our purpose work is broader than the particular job we hold right now, we open up some new possibilities, while also avoiding some of the pitfalls that can come from tying our identity and self-worth too closely to a position or title.

And back to the problem with "work-life balance," which is typically used to contrast our paycheck work with our life. The contrast for paycheck work is nonwork; it is not life. And it is our work and our nonwork that are in alliance, mutually supporting each other for the holistic health of the individual: our whole lives. But there is no contrasting idea for purpose work, because plenty of nonwork activities (like time with family and friends) can be a part of one's mission and purpose. Indeed, it is our personal relationships that add the most meaning to our lives.

So while there is no one word to embody the contrast in our lives for purpose work, there *are* things we can recognize that fall outside of our missions. Recognizing this, being able to discern whether an opportunity aligns with our mission, whether it will enhance our alliance or not, frees us to know when to say "yes" and when to say "no, that's not my (purpose) work." And declining an opportunity is not a value judgment in an essential sense: it doesn't mean that the thing isn't important! But if you know that an opportunity falls outside of both your paycheck work and your purpose work, it's clearly not the kind of work for you to do right now.

It's hard to overstate the value of this kind of clarity. In the world of organizations and businesses, role definitions can be critical, so that everyone on the team working towards a goal understands the scope of their responsibilities and their authority. The same is true in our lives! Being clear on what is a part of our mission and what is not both frees and empowers us.

I will accept responsibility for many things not part of my paycheck work but which are part of my purpose work: board service, committee work, offering pro bono advice and consultations for certain organizations, comforting a grieving friend, offering childcare to a loved one, volunteering in my community. And then there are plenty of opportunities that I turn down, because they don't fall within the current scope of my purpose work, at least not right now. The scope of a person's purpose work will also change over time; that's why the correct positions of work and nonwork in an aligned life are relative. Raising children may become a critically important part of your purpose work, but you can't prioritize this raising of children before you have them. Our purpose work will evolve over the course of our lives. Having clarity on *what I am here to do and be right now* offers us freedom, in a way that none of my "better balance plans" ever could.

Alignment means honoring ourselves. It means not doing things because we think we are "supposed to" but choosing our activities because they fit within our purpose work, and so they honor our life's energy. It's about being confident that we are right where we're supposed to be, doing the thing we're supposed to be doing, and then letting go of the rest.

So it's important to consider: At this point in your life, what is your purpose work? Your mission? For most of us, it likely includes the activities for which we are compensated. But for you, does it include more than that?

There's an argument here that needs acknowledging, too. Some might say that it can be considered an incredibly privileged position to think of paycheck work as part of purpose work, as the place where income is generated *and* meaning is found. Such an argument, though, assumes that for some jobs or occupations, finding meaning might be impossible. I would agree that there is nothing inherently wrong with someone who does not feel this overlap, as would be the case for someone who goes off to spend hours at work in order to have the income to live their lives, but who doesn't feel any sort of mission or calling attached. (This is, of course, provided that such a person is not miserable, the work is not unethical, and the income is sufficient. Which means I also believe some societal shifts to promote greater equity in the workplace are needed.)

In addition to asking what exactly *is* our work, I would also suggest that we ask another question: why *can't* there be personal meaning found in all types of work? Drawing on the Montessori principle of the nobility of work, as long as the work is not harmful to self or others, it seems problematic to me to suggest that there can be no inherent meaning or value found in all types of work. Dr. Martin Luther King Jr.'s exhortation to students at Barratt Junior High School in Philadelphia had a similar view. He said, "If it falls your lot to be a street sweeper, sweep streets like Michelangelo painted pictures, sweep streets like Beethoven composed music… sweep streets so well that all the hosts of heaven and earth will have to pause and say: 'Here lived a great street sweeper who swept his job well.'"

Understanding the terms "paycheck work" (paid employment) and "purpose work" (cosmic task; what I am on this planet to do and be right now) gives us a way to reconcile Montessori's ideas about work with society's (often confusing and conflicting) advice about work. It also can provide the start of a roadmap for aligning or realigning our life's mosaic. If something falls outside of both my paycheck work and my purpose work, it's not a mosaic piece for me to hold right now!

CHAPTER 2 SECOND PERIOD: THE PRACTICE

Writing Activity

Make a first draft (it can be as messy and imperfect as it needs to be now) of what you'd describe as your purpose work, your cosmic task. I like to think of this as who you are here to be and what you are here to do at this time in your life.

Reflection Questions

- Do you see a lot of overlap between your paycheck work and your purpose work?

- What makes your work personal for you? When is that joyful? When is it hard?

- What times in your life have you seen your overall well-being positively impacted by your work? What times in your life have you seen your overall well-being negatively impacted by your work?

- What times in your life have you seen your work positively impacted by other (nonwork) pieces of your life? What times in your life have you seen your work negatively impacted by nonwork pieces?

- Are any of the 10 Montessori ideas about work already a part of your perspective?

- Are there any of the 10 ideas that are outside of how you usually think about work?

- Are there any that you'd like to adopt to change your mindset about the term "work"?

- Are there any that you'd like to bring into your workplace?

- Thinking of the butterfly effect from chaos theory (that poetic idea that a butterfly flapping its wings might cause a tornado or hurricane on the other side of the world), can you name someone you've never met but who nevertheless impacted your life in an important way?

- Can you hypothesize about how your life and work could ripple out beyond the people you directly impact?

CHAPTER 2 THIRD PERIOD: THE APPLICATION

Paycheck Work and Purpose Work

Getting clear on our paycheck work and our purpose work helps us make important decisions about our life mosaic, where to spend our finite time on this planet. Is there work you are currently doing, something that is taking up space in your life mosaic, that falls outside of **both** your paycheck work and your purpose work? If you've invited a valued other along your alignment journey, talk through these ideas with them. And then together, start making a plan for what it would look like to let that work go—ideally with a timeline if it's not something you can drop right away—because it's just not your work to do!

3

You Don't Have to Quit Your Job (But You Might Want To)

I HAVE TWO BRILLIANT SISTERS, both younger than me. The youngest one, Abby, called me up one October day. I knew she had been having "a little hard time," as we would often say to each other when things felt heavy in our lives. The hospital where she had worked for the past seven years was (again) in a season of being short-staffed, and it was hard to see when the load might lighten. Abby had been sharing concerns with me recently about nursing burnout and not wanting her own emotional exhaustion to impede her ability to care for her oncology patients.

For sure, Abby gave a lot of herself to her work. She had climbed the clinical ladder, providing service and leadership as well as mentoring to other nurses, including a revamp of the chemo training all nurses completed at her hospital. In only her fourth year at the hospital, Abby had even been recognized with a special award for excellence in oncology nursing practice. But beyond all her accomplishments, Abby was most proud of her ability to be truly present with her patients, to see and support their full humanity as they worked through severe health needs. Abby's unit was for stem cell transplant and acute oncology patients, who often had extended and recurring stays at the hospital, and Abby often met them in some of the hardest moments of their lives. And I could see the evidence of Abby's gift in the thank-you notes plastered all over the fridge in her apartment. Abby had so many, usually from patients themselves, but also sometimes from their surviving family members.

Because people feel it when you care.

And Abby didn't want to lose her ability to care.

Today, though, things had moved beyond having "a little hard time." When I picked up the phone, there were none of the usual pleasantries to warm up the conversation. Instead, she called me by my rarely used family nickname, with a voice that sounded small and unsure. "Kates..." Her voice cracked as she trailed off. "How do you know when it's time to quit your job?"

Your Current and Desired Life Mosaic

If you're at the point that Abby was—seriously considering leaving work that you find meaningful and important—you already know that you're out of alignment. The work pieces of your life mosaic are showing cracks and are not supporting the stability of the whole. You don't have a healthy alliance among work and nonwork pieces.

And maybe, like Abby, you've been collecting advice about what you should do next. Whether it's time to walk away from work that you love, because it's just become too much. Maybe it's even the reason that you're reading this book.

One thing I've noticed when I talk to former teachers is that many of them have a wistful tone when they talk about the work they left behind. They usually feel convinced that they made the right decision for themselves, their families, and maybe even their bank accounts, but more often than not, they also report that being with kids is something they truly loved—and still miss. Many of them say things like "if only [whatever barrier got in the way] had been different, I'd still be teaching." This has always broken my heart a little bit, because first, I know what a life-changing difference a great teacher can make for kids, and it's a huge loss to students when amazing teachers feel that they need to leave their jobs. And second, because we only have one tiny and treasured life, leaving a job that we find meaningful and rewarding can leave a real void in our lives. So, in the same way I'm always sorry to hear someone share about a deep love they had (with a person) that didn't work out, I hate to see folks walk away from careers that mean so much to them. Finding meaningful work, like finding love, can be one of life's greatest gifts. Not something to take for granted.

But Abby's position had become untenable. And maybe yours is, too.

So the only way out, as they say, is through. And here's the bad news: You're the only one who can decide if you need a change in your current employment. But the good news is that you're the only one that you need! You don't need anyone else to determine if you need to make a change! It starts with a deep dive into your life's current and desired mosaic.

This can be hard work, because we have to look at our whole life mosaic, including the pieces that aren't as shiny.

Sometimes, when work isn't working, we take the drastic route: a new title, a new job, or even a new career. And there's nothing wrong with change; we grow, we learn new skills, we continue the adventure called life. But if we're creating change for the sake of change, if we're throwing spaghetti against the wall to see what sticks, we need a more precise approach. We only have one life mosaic, and changing out some of our work pieces without addressing our whole life mosaic may not be the magic fix we expect.

So first, we need to go back to the idea of purpose work, your cosmic task. What are you here to do and be right now? (Because remember, your work is so much bigger than just your job!) How does your job, your paycheck work, fit into your bigger purpose work? How much overlap do you want there to be between your paycheck work and your purpose work?

It's important to be realistic here. Because while I believe that our life mosaics can expand, and that your you-ness, your essence, is infinite, your time and your energy are not. (Though there *are* ways to reconsider our time and to renew our energy... more on that in Chapter 7.)

And while our mosaics can grow, we still have to make choices about what to prioritize and when. The simple fact is, our lives have seasons. Our days have rhythms. So all our important mosaic pieces can receive attention, but not at the same time. And prioritizing one piece means deprioritizing another, at least for the moment.

That doesn't mean that if you choose to spend an hour on a hobby, on a piece of work, or on a call with a friend, instead of giving 100 percent of your focus for that hour to your children, that you value your children less than that thing. Making choices based on our priorities has to be about the big picture. Your family pieces may be the most precious parts of your life mosaic, but they're still not the only pieces, and it's okay—no, *essential*—to devote time and energy to your other pieces as well. (And not just the pieces you *have* to attend to, but also the pieces you *want* to attend to.) This is a hard lesson sometimes for givers, because time with loved ones can be so precious. (What is the expression about raising children, that "the days are long, but the years are short"?) We know that time with loved ones can be fleeting. But also, there's no real "end" to these priorities. You can check certain tasks off, sure, reading a story to your children if that's a practice that's important to you, or family dinner. But you can't say "great, met my quota of kids for the day/week/month, so I'll spend the rest of my time on other things." In theory, we could each spend 100 percent of our waking minutes attending to our children, but that's neither realistic nor healthy for anybody.

You might also consider, what does your work give back to you? What do you want it to provide in your life? Getting clear on how your paycheck work fits into your purpose work, and how much overlap you want there to be, can be incredibly empowering. We are the ones who get to shape our life mosaic. We get to decide where and how the pieces fit. You are the only one you need.

When Work Isn't Working: An Honest Assessment

There are research-based indicators of thriving in the workplace that can help you assess your paycheck work. In fact, because organizations definitely have a vested interest in figuring out how to support human thriving at work, there's a robust body of evidence on the topic.

A 2017 review of literature on human thriving noted that, in addition to family support, positive attachment, and trusting relationships, our work environment can have a significant impact on our overall thriving. First, and not surprisingly, our place of work can impact our thriving via the quality of support felt by colleagues and supervisors. But also work can provide another key enabler of human thriving: an environment with an appropriate challenge level. Having this appropriate challenge level (the work is interesting and hard enough, without being overwhelming) can support feelings of autonomy, competence, and relatedness (positive relationships with others, feeling that you make a difference), which can promote feelings of accomplishment and growth. Researchers recommend clear goals and feedback, opportunities for self-expression, flexibility to meet human needs, along with a supportive community and meaningful work. (Sounds like a Montessori classroom to me!)

So if you're in the place where Abby was on the day of that phone call, it's time to take stock of whether your paycheck work is living up to its potential. It's time for an honest assessment, because once we can pinpoint where the challenges lie, we are empowered to focus on a solution.

I created the following assessment to help us think through to what extent our work is or isn't working for us. Unless otherwise stated, consider your paycheck work over the last three to six months.

1. I feel a lot of anxiety or sadness the night before starting my workweek or several consecutive shifts.

   - 5 less than 10% of the time
   - 4 10–25% of the time
   - 3 25–50% of the time
   - 2 50–75% of the time
   - 1 75–90% of the time
   - 0 90–100% of the time

2. I have colleagues who make work joyful; we laugh with and support each other.

   - 0 less than 10% of the time
   - 1 0–25% of the time
   - 2 25–50% of the time
   - 3 50–75% of the time
   - 4 75–90% of the time
   - 5 90–100% of the time

3. At some point on a day off, I find myself resentful that I am not doing the things I want to because I am either recovering from my work or doing more work to catch up/get ahead.

   - 5 less than 10% of the time
   - 4 10–25% of the time
   - 3 25–50% of the time
   - 2 50–75% of the time
   - 1 75–90% of the time
   - 0 90–100% of the time

4 I feel that I can successfully manage most of the challenges that I face in my work.

- 0 less than 10% of the time
- 1 10–25% of the time
- 2 5–50% of the time
- 3 50–75% of the time
- 4 75–90% of the time
- 5 90–100% of the time

5 I enjoy thinking about or planning for my work.

- 0 less than 10% of the time
- 1 10–25% of the time
- 2 25–50% of the time
- 3 50–75% of the time
- 4 75–90% of the time
- 5 90–100% of the time

6 I generally receive positive feedback, appreciation, or recognition for my work.

- 0 once or twice per year or less
- 1 once every month or two
- 2 once or twice per month
- 3 most workweeks
- 4 more than once per workweek
- 5 pretty much every day that I work

7 I feel confident that at least 40% of the time I spend at work is contributing to making the world a better place in some way.
   - 0   once or twice per year or less
   - 1   once every month or two
   - 2   once or twice per month
   - 3   most workweeks
   - 4   more than once per workweek
   - 5   pretty much every day that I work

8 My work is a source of friction in my personal relationships.
   - 5   once or twice per year or less
   - 4   once every month or two
   - 3   once or twice per month
   - 2   most workweeks
   - 1   more than once per workweek
   - 0   pretty much every day I work

9 I know where to get support at work when I need help managing my responsibilities.
   - 0   less than 10% of the time
   - 1   10–25% of the time
   - 2   25–50% of the time
   - 3   50–75% of the time
   - 4   75–90% of the time
   - 5   90–100% of the time

10 I sleep as well as I usually do the night before starting my workweek or several consecutive shifts.

- 0 less than 10% of the time
- 1 10–25% of the time
- 2 25–50% of the time
- 3 50–75% of the time
- 4 75–90% of the time
- 5 90–100% of the time

11 I feel that I have or can ask for opportunities to grow and try new things at work.

- 0 less than 10% of the time
- 1 10–25% of the time
- 2 25–50% of the time
- 3 50–75% of the time
- 4 75–90% of the time
- 5 90–100% of the time

12 If I find myself thinking about or planning for work, it's enjoyable:

- 0 less than 10% of the time
- 1 10–25% of the time
- 2 25–50% of the time
- 3 50–75% of the time
- 4 75–90% of the time
- 5 90–100% of the time

13 Depending on my type of work:

- If I average five or more days of work per week, I have energy to manage my nonwork goals and responsibilities (such as exercise, healthy eating, paying bills on time, and returning personal phone calls) through the week; I don't have to save all these elements for my weekends.

- If I work longer shifts for an average of less than five days per week, I have energy to manage all my nonwork goals and responsibilities (such as exercise, healthy eating, paying bills on time, and returning personal phone calls) on all my days off.

    0   less than 10% of the time
    1   10–25% of the time
    2   25–50% of the time
    3   50–75% of the time
    4   75–90% of the time
    5   90–100% of the time

14 My most important people are proud of and support the work I do.

    0   less than 10% of the time
    1   10–25% of the time
    2   25–50% of the time
    3   50–75% of the time
    4   75–90% of the time
    5   90–100% of the time

15 Time generally passes quickly for me when I am working.

    0   less than 10% of the time
    1   10–25% of the time
    2   25–50% of the time
    3   50–75% of the time
    4   75–90% of the time
    5   90–100% of the time

16 I feel like I am generally good at the work that I do.

0   less than 10% of the time
1   10–25% of the time
2   25–50% of the time
3   50–75% of the time
4   75–90% of the time
5   90–100% of the time

17 I feel physically and psychologically safe at work.

0   less than 10% of the time
1   10–25% of the time
2   25–50% of the time
3   50–75% of the time
4   75–90% of the time
5   90–100% of the time

Scoring

Before you tally, take a hard look at that last one, number 17. Everyone has the right to feel safe at work. Regardless of your other scores, number 17 might be the dealbreaker. It's time to find another option if you're in a truly toxic or unsafe workplace. More on that at the end of the chapter.

That said, tally the rest of your scores and use the descriptions below to get a sense of where you are right now. Try on the descriptions; see if they fit for you. It's possible that you might find a different description that fits you better, and that's because some questions, and your responses to them, may be more important to you than others or may have a bigger impact on your life's healthy alliance.

It's also important to realize that alignment is a process and not a permanent destination. How you feel about things today might be different from a week ago or a month from now. But, if we can gain clarity on where we are, and to what extent our paycheck work isn't serving our life's alignment, we gain important clues about how to move forward. This is brave work!

Score set one, 0–34 range: *There's a major problem here. It's time to unpack what's going on.* If your overall score was in the 0–34 range, then your work and nonwork pieces are definitely not supporting one another right now. And while no job is perfect, there are some major elements missing that are required in order to thrive. Assuming that emotional or physical safety is not the issue, you only need to find a first step. It is time to get curious about what you most want your work and nonwork to look like. Where were your scores the lowest? What would change those scores? And are there any brighter spots that you can build on?

Score set two, 35–51 range: *Things could definitely be better. But there might be some bright spots, too.* If your total score was in the 35–51 range, then your work and nonwork have elements of misalignment that need your attention. This is completely normal, at different times, for almost everyone. Most of us did not grow up with a framework that can support a healthy life alignment; we've absorbed a lot of messages about the role our work *should* play in our lives or what our personal values *should* be. But alignment is about uncovering our own truths and crafting a life of meaning and thriving that works for us. In the next chapter, we'll take the first steps of the alignment process, so that we can discern where we need to make some changes. For now, you might note where your scores were higher and lower, to see if you can find any trends.

Score set three, 52–68 range: *Things seem mostly good. But there's always room for improvement.* If the sum of your answers falls in the 52–68 range, then your work and nonwork show signs of alignment. Hurray! There are many elements of your work that are healthy and contributing to your overall well-being. You've got some of the bigger pieces under control, but there appears to still be some room to tweak and improve. For you, small adjustments might have a huge impact on your alignment. You might also need to really tune into yourself to unpack what might be behind the lower scores. Looking for any trends that appear where your answers were higher or lower can be helpful, too.

Score set four, 69–85 range: *Congratulations! Your work is supporting your life's healthy alignment.* If your answers brought you to the 69–85 range, then your work and nonwork are mostly aligned. Remember, too, that alignment is a process, not a permanent destination. Change is inevitable in our lives, and we all have different seasons. The good news is that maintaining our alignment through every stage is possible.

Getting to a Decision: Should I Stay or Should I Go?

There's no way around it, walking away from a profession you love can have a big impact on your life mosaic. And while there are definitely times when leaving a position or career is the right call, most of the time we don't have to give it all up. We don't have to change professions, taking this nuclear option, unless we truly *want* to. Even if we feel that we've been consumed by the job, we don't necessarily have to walk away from every part of the work we love to feel like a whole person again. In fact, unless we're truly ready, walking away from our work can have major downsides for us as well, and these potential downsides are worth considering.

First, we may find that leaving is not the solution we thought it would be. If we're still pursuing the myth of balance, we may just find ourselves in another setting with the exact same problems. Worse, if we have traded our meaningful profession for one that we thought would feel more "balanced," we may find ourselves with the same frustrations but less meaning in our lives. Jon Kabat-Zinn popularized the saying "wherever you go, there you are," and it's an important concept for our life's alignment. In other words, you're still the same person, even if the job changes, because our pieces are all connected.

Second, we chose this work for a reason. If we still love the work, and still *want* to do this work, leaving it can create a major hole in our lives. As I shared before, I've spoken with plenty of former teachers who are still wistful, even after many years away from teaching. They wanted to stay in the classroom but couldn't see a viable path forward, and they're sad (and sometimes bitter) that they felt leaving the profession was their only option. We may miss the work itself.

Third, we chose this work as a way to bring *our* unique talents, experiences, and skills to make a difference in the world. When our paycheck work is a part of our purpose work, it has deep connections to who we are and what we feel we are meant to offer the world. Walking away completely, then, can feel like an abandonment of our very selves. We may miss who we are and how we come alive in our work.

Fourth, and the main reason I don't think you should walk away from a profession you know you still love is that you are a unique gift to the world. Your life and your work matter, and the ripple effects of your work, the lives you touch, are incalculable. Losing you won't just impact your current colleagues, clients, students, parishioners, or patients and *their* networks, it will also impact all the future lives you and your future colleagues, clients, students, parishioners, or patients could have touched. You are the butterfly.

I'm passionate about helping caring professionals who make the world a better place learn how to joyfully remain in their chosen professions for as long as *they* want to, because we need each other. I want great teachers for every child, now and forever. I want great medical professionals for when we all inevitably need healthcare. I want spiritual advisors, social workers, and activists who can stay the course to keep ushering in a more peaceful, just, equitable, and sustainable world that works for everyone. These are remarkable people. *You* are a remarkable person. When such a person leaves their profession forever, abandoning a part of their purpose work, the cost is incalculable.

So you might want to quit your job, and that's okay. You might want to separate your paycheck work and your purpose work, or you might want to find another position that also feels in line with your purpose work. I have experienced all three shifts in my working life.

But if you're not sure, if you're still reading because you just know that *something* needs to change, then we need to have a way to recognize to what extent work isn't working, so that we can make the appropriate changes. We may not need a sledgehammer and a massive remodel of our lives if a screwdriver can tighten a few things to bring alignment.

When Abby called me, asking how to tell if it was time to quit her job, she knew something had to change. Maybe you're in that same place right now, too. Or maybe you've been there in the past, or you want to know how to avoid getting to that uncomfortable place in the future. Abby had a lot to weigh in making her decision, just like anyone who cares deeply about their work.

The good news is, most of the time, we don't have to completely abandon the work we (at least once) loved, that we trained for, and that we were excited to land. When we learn how to bring our whole lives into alignment, when our work and our nonwork are in a supportive alliance, new possibilities open up for us to do our work and make a difference in the lives of others, without losing ourselves in the process. It is possible to bring thriving to our whole lives, including our work. Abby did, I did, and you can, too.

But there's an important caveat. I mentioned briefly that sometimes work can be a toxic place, and when that's true, leaving is usually the right answer. I've mentioned it in the scoring of the assessment above, but I want to be crystal clear here that *no one should stay in an environment where they are emotionally, psychologically, or physically in danger.* This includes the obvious and illegal racial and sexual harassment at work, as well as the more subtle psychological abuse: shaming, fear as a method of control, microaggressions, or other problematic scenarios. So, although I believe that the best option for a toxic environment would be for it to improve via accountability and repair of harm, so that the cycle doesn't continue, if you are the victim in such a workplace, it is not your responsibility to bring these changes about. Please do not stay in a setting where the culture or actions of others diminishes your full humanity.

CHAPTER 3 SECOND PERIOD: THE PRACTICE

Writing Activity

Take the assessment if you only skimmed it before, and make a list of where your scores were notably higher or lower. What can these scores reveal about your working life? Do they indicate any urgent changes that are needed?

Reflection Questions

- How does your job, your paycheck work, fit into your purpose work right now?

- How much overlap do you *want* there to be between your paycheck work and your purpose work?

- What does your work give back to you?

- What do you *want* your work to provide in your life?

- Researchers suggest that our work is most likely to have a positive impact on us when we have clear goals and feedback, opportunities for self-expression, flexibility to meet our human needs, work that feels meaningful, and a supportive community. Which of these are strengths in your current position? Which could be improved?

CHAPTER 3 THIRD PERIOD: THE APPLICATION

Should I Stay or Should I Go?

As I wrote in this chapter, I'm passionate about helping caring professionals who make the world a better place learn how to joyfully remain in their chosen professions for as long as *they* want to, because we need each other. *You* are a remarkable person, and just like the butterfly effect, your impact on the world is incalculable. As I've said several times now: your work matters, but please remember that *you* matter more.

So your decision to stay or go might not be crystal clear yet, but if you took the assessment and did the second period practice, you are probably getting a better idea. So let's apply that idea.

If it is time to leave your current position (and again, please do not stay in an environment where you are emotionally, psychologically, or physically in danger), your third period application here is to make that exit plan. Maybe you're ready to draft a resignation letter, or maybe you just want to map out a timeline of your departure, including when and how you'll research and decide on what comes next. Maybe you're going to spend the rest of the evening updating your résumé and professional profiles, or contacting a counselor (maybe a therapist, or maybe a career counselor) to discuss your options. Leaving can certainly be fraught with unknowns, and your financial situation must also be taken into consideration. But if your deepest knowing says that it's time to leave, then it's *at least* time to make a real plan.

On the other hand, as I've shared, leaving isn't always the answer we think it might be. So if you're feeling out of alignment due to your work, but it's *not* crystal clear that you definitely need to have an exit strategy yet, your third period application here is to talk through (maybe with your valued other... let's keep this conversation going!) what your current and future metrics or dealbreakers might be. You might consider the following:

- What needs to improve for you to feel confident that this is a healthy place for you to do your work? Is there a timeline by which you'd want to see improvement?

- Are there ways to minimize the parts of your work that are having a negative impact on you? What would that look like, and what support would you need from others to make this happen?

- Do you need or want to focus more on what you can celebrate or appreciate about your work? What would help provide this kind of reframe for you?

And finally, if you're *not* feeling that work is causing significant misalignment in your life, hooray! Your application of this confirmation is to continue to enjoy leaning into your work, prioritizing and building on the strengths, while staying attuned to any parts that could still be improved.

4

Finding Alignment, Part I: Noticing Our Work-Life Alliance

WHEN CHRIS NORTON was a freshman in college, a football tackle gone amiss separated the vertebrae of his spine and damaged his spinal cord. He was told that the damage to his spinal cord had rendered him quadriplegic, and that only 3 percent of patients with injuries like his would ever regain any sensation or movement below the neck. This is the kind of moment that changes a life forever.

The film *7 Yards* documents Chris's journey from the moment of his injury through his recovery, and the viewer can't help but cheer for Chris as he determines what matters most to him and pursues his goals with hope and determination. We see Chris take his very first steps to receive his college diploma, and with continued hard work, he goes on to walk seven yards down the aisle of his wedding, with his wife Emily by his side.

But this story is told primarily in Chris's own words, and he doesn't sugarcoat it. This injury caused a major shift in identity for Chris, and nothing about his recovery process was easy. Early in the film, we witness the terror and pain of Chris's first days in the hospital. And we see that the first step in actual treatment for Chris, after testing his (lack of) sensation in the body, was to put him in traction to realign his spine.

When Chris was knocked down hard, when his life changed forever, getting his body back into alignment was the first step. Physical alignment of his spine was a prerequisite to his healing journey, necessary to see what kind of recovery might even be possible.

To be sure, confronting a possible quadriplegia diagnosis is uniquely devastating in its own right, and I was deeply moved by Chris's story. I was also struck by a parallel. In watching the film, I saw just how essential alignment of the spinal cord is for full expression of bodily movement and function. And I think the alignment of our lives is also essential for full expression of our human potential and thriving. In the same way that Chris's need for spinal alignment was the first step towards recovery, we, too, need to look at alignment, but of our lives, as a first step towards remedying our circumstances when we are no longer thriving in the work we love. In fact, I think Chris's story has a lot to teach us about alignment.

Alignment is a process, not a permanent destination. As lovely as it would be to finally arrive forever, the fact is, we'll be aligning and realigning our lives for the rest of our lives, because our circumstances are in a perpetual state of change. And in many ways, this is a beautiful thing! The very process of alignment requires us to take a breath, to pay attention to what's really going on, and to notice what is deep inside us. We can't align our lives without paying attention to our lives, and the film character Ferris Bueller was right when he said, "Life moves pretty fast." But not only should we look around ourselves every once in a while, as Ferris recommends, we should also look inside ourselves to make sure we aren't missing something. The attention we can offer ourselves is always a worthwhile investment. *We* are the constant in our own lives.

I like to think of the alignment process as two parts of a whole: part "habit" (noticing when our needs and most important wants aren't being honored by our work or nonwork), part "thinking tool" (the questions we ask once we've noticed that we're out of alignment). We'll find that as we build our alignment habits, realigning can happen faster, sometimes even automatically. We won't need as many massive course corrections. And the process frees us from the grind of perfectionism, because alignment isn't about having it all together. It's about noticing and honoring ourselves. After all, we're going to live with ourselves for our entire lives.

To start, let's go back to our two definitions of "alignment" from Chapter 1.

Mosaics and Alliances: Two Definitions of Alignment

noun: *alignment*

1 arrangement in a straight line, or in correct or appropriate relative positions.

2 a position of agreement or alliance.

We've talked about all the pieces of our life mosaic being arranged in their "correct or appropriate relative positions," and that these pieces can be placed in such a way to support and bolster one another, like the beautiful mosaic floor of the Pantheon: a healthy "agreement or alliance" among our work and nonwork pieces.

In healthcare, the "therapeutic alliance" or "working alliance" between provider and patient has been shown to have an important impact on both mental and physical health outcomes. This alliance is all about building a bond that comes from trust and confidence that the activities or tasks of the provider will bring the patient or client closer to their goals. The two parties aren't in opposition to one another, and they respect the realm of one another. The provider can't make the health outcomes just happen; the client has to take the actual steps. And the client needs the outside perspective and unique expertise of the provider, both for the practical next steps and for the moral support and encouragement. But working together in a trusting relationship, the synergy between the two parties has been linked to much greater outcomes than if the alliance was weak. It's this kind of productive alliance and synergy we want to have among our work and nonwork pieces.

The movie *7 Yards* also documents a few moments where Chris's therapeutic alliances made a huge difference for him. The first was an early-morning doctor, just checking his vitals, who came upon Chris in one of his dark nights of the soul. Chris was alone in a hospital bed at an hour when the rest of the world was still sleeping, crying and wondering what was next for his life. This doctor got down to eye level and asked Chris to look her in the eyes. She told him she was from Wisconsin, and she asked if he knew anyone from Wisconsin. When he admitted that he didn't, she told him firmly that "people from Wisconsin don't tell lies" and then went on to let him know that he was going to have an incredible recovery. Chris spoke about how, sometimes, all it takes is an encouraging word at the right time to change your perspective. Because although plenty of others had expressed their well-wishes and encouragement for a full recovery, it was *this* doctor who helped Chis to believe in his own possibility.

But she wasn't the only one. While Chris spent over four years at the Mayo Clinic with a grueling rehabilitation regimen, when he returned home to continue his therapy, he learned about another therapist who had invented a special method for spinal patients. So he and his girlfriend set off to work with this new trainer, with the audacious goal of taking his first steps while walking across the stage to receive his college diploma. Chris placed his trust in this trainer to know just how hard to push; he endured grueling rehabilitation workouts and exercises every day, with no days off. This therapeutic alliance made all the difference for Chris in keeping him on track to meet his unbelievable goals, goals that most doctors never thought could become a reality.

And Chris had alignment in his life. Not only was the therapeutic alliance between him and his caregivers strong, but also if his work was recovery and his nonwork was everything else, pieces from both sides of this life alliance came together to support his holistic functioning and well-being. It's pretty easy to see Chris's nonwork supports throughout the movie. First, he spoke extensively of a personal faith that brought comfort through the challenges, believing that there was a reason and a higher purpose for his life's calling. Second, his personal dispositions of optimism, determination, and perseverance cannot be understated. Not that he never felt demoralized or pessimistic; Chris had some dark nights of the soul, too. But overwhelmingly, he stayed positive about and committed to his recovery work. Third, his human support network rallied around him in impressive ways. No doubt these humans were a big part of supporting and maintaining his positive dispositions.

In the early days of being in the hospital, his immediate family were his greatest supporters: his parents and two sisters, especially in the ways they encouraged him and were determined to keep his spirits up and believe in his capabilities for recovery. Later, his football teammates showed up in incredible ways: with regular visits to see him in the hospital, but then in providing round-the-clock care and support when Chris decided to go back to school and continue earning his degree. His football family showed up like true brothers, taking care of Chris's every need, from moving him in and out of his wheelchair, helping him have some "normal friend time," helping with personal grooming and dressing, and even taking turns sharing a bed with Chris so they could keep him safe during any muscle spasms or issues in the night. And then when Chris met Emily after his accident, he found in her a partner to support the rest of his growth and development, and the family and life they built together was extraordinary to see.

It's clear that if Chris's work was recovery, the nonwork pieces of his life showed up in important ways to support him, via his faith, his personal dispositions, and his supportive relationships. It's also clear that Chris had environmental supports in the form of access to the Mayo Clinic and some of the best rehabilitation equipment and experts anywhere on the planet, experts who also believed in him.

But in watching Chris share his story, I believe that this hard work of recovery was a support to his nonwork side in important ways, too. It's hard to argue that his relationships with friends and family didn't deepen—when your college buddies literally carry you around, help with personal grooming, and even share your bed, a new level of bonding was present. His relationship with Emily progressed from first date to engagement to marriage to family-building in a way that cannot be separated from the work they both put into his recovery.

In the movie Chris also speaks of finding meaning in his recovery work, feeling that his work matters and has a higher purpose. He describes wanting his life to be an inspiration to others, to make a difference for the world, and to help others facing seemingly insurmountable challenges. Chris's website (chrisnorton.org) reiterates a truth we all know, at least intellectually: We all get knocked down sometimes. His work, his recovery, taught him lessons about life that most would not have learned in their early twenties. And now his work continues: a charitable foundation to support people with spinal cord and neuromuscular disabilities, a free "wheelchair camp" for youth and families, and a speaking career dedicated to helping others "push past life's challenges."

I don't know Chris personally; I can't speak for whether he feels alignment in his life or how often he feels the need to realign. But I can say that his story showed a powerful illustration of the importance of both literal and metaphorical alignment in our lives. And while our work may not be personal recovery from a catastrophic injury, we still want our work and our nonwork to be in an alliance, working together in support of our own human thriving. And we want these pieces in their correct relative positions, a beautiful mosaic for this time in our lives.

We'll talk more about creating a developmental container for ourselves—what it looks like and what it takes—in Chapter 6, but here, let's take a deeper dive into the habit part of the alignment process. Because when we build our alignment habits, we find that it's possible to thrive in our whole lives, while still also making a difference in the lives of others.

The Process of Alignment: Wants, Needs, and Loops

I'll say it again, because while it would be nice to align our lives once and for all, it just doesn't work that way. Finding and maintaining our alignment really is a process, not a permanent destination. We will be continually reflecting on the alignment of our lives, making adjustments as life brings us new changes and challenges. As we learn to align, we can also consider how big changes are likely to affect our alignment, we can notice what tendencies we have that serve our alignment (or don't), and we can have conversations with valued others about what we need for alignment in our own lives. And maybe, just maybe, we can support the healthy alignment of their lives as well.

To keep a healthy alliance among our work and our non-work pieces, it can help to consider the parts of our lives in the way that elite athletes do, who know that work and non-work are equally important to their optimal functioning. An Olympian knows that periods of maximum effort on the field/track/water/slopes requires periods of maximum rest and recovery away from the arena. The eating, sleeping, physical therapy, stretching, warm-ups, cool-downs, psychological care, and even team bonding are not extraneous "nice to do if you have the time" parts of life. No, they're all essential components for maximum performance. As whole people, they have to nurture all parts of themselves and all parts of their lives.

In my life, I'm pretty dedicated to sleep. And while I sometimes wish that I didn't need *quite* as much sleep as I seem to, embracing and honoring my sleep schedule has been a game changer for me. I'm naturally more of an early riser, and I absolutely love the early morning hours. I love the quiet, the sense of hopefulness I feel when I consider the possibilities of the day, the warm tea or coffee that clears some of the mist from my sleepy brain. I love morning light, how happy it makes me to see the dawn creep in and coax the neighborhood to life. When I travel, I care almost as much about official sunrise times as I do time zones. I also know that I am happier and healthier when I have this morning time for myself, before I need to face the world. And I can do my best thinking, my best writing, and my best creative work in the mornings. Yet to have the morning time I want, it's my end-of-day routines that matter most. Having a good morning means having a ritual for ending my workday, and not checking my work email after hours, so I can be fully present to other parts of my life. It means eating my evening meal early enough and with food and drink choices that won't negatively impact my sleep. And it means making my way towards the bed an hour or so before I hope to be asleep. While I'm not perfect with my sleep schedule, I am serious about it. I treat getting enough sleep like an athlete might; not as a "nice to do if you have the time" thing, but as an essential component of my whole life. I know that doing so has kept me healthier than I ever was before and has contributed to my own maximum performance in my life.

So our alignment is driven by two facets: what we most want out of our one tiny and treasured life and what we need.

The first driver of our alignment, what we want, is a function of our core values and our individual wiring. We all have things that drive us, that make life most satisfying. And there is no shortage of assessments and tests that many people have found helpful for determining their drivers, from Love Languages, to Enneagram or Myers-Briggs personality tests, to CliftonStrengths or VIA Character Strengths profiles. While I find some assessments and results more helpful than others, I appreciate that they hold up a mirror to the patterns in my actions and thoughts, *and* that they help me remember not everyone is wired just like me. Since our values will differ, so, too, will our life mosaics. And there is such richness in this diversity!

Self-improvement experts, like Stephen Covey, have long advocated for personal mission statements. Taking the time to discern (and discuss with people who know you well) what your deepest drivers are, and what you, as a unique individual on this planet, want out of your life. Just remember that your mission can evolve over time as well!

The second driver of our alignment is our needs. Humans have certain needs, and developmental psychologist Abraham Maslow gave them a hierarchy that humans move through; perhaps you've seen the famous "hierarchy of needs" pyramid image. In Maslow's initial model of the hierarchy, physiological needs are the most basic, followed by safety and security. Then our needs for belonging and love can be met, followed by needs for self-esteem. Finally, if all other levels of needs can be met, humans can move to fulfilling their needs for self-actualization.

Psychologists Richard Ryan and Edward Deci's self-determination theory (SDT) is another powerful lens for thinking about human needs and motivation, especially as we consider our work. Ryan and Deci posit that human beings have three basic psychological needs of autonomy, competence, and relatedness. Having these needs met in life is critical, but having these needs met in our paycheck work can also be a major driver of our overall well-being, as the thriving research that I referenced in Chapter 3 has indicated.

The actual alignment process is circular, a loop. It starts with noticing that the alliance among our work and nonwork pieces is not operating as we would like it to, that our critical needs and wants are not being met. As a result, we are not functioning holistically where all parts of the alliance further our thriving. The process is circular because it begins and ends with this noticing. Intuitively, this makes sense since we can't make a change if we don't notice the problem, or if we can't pinpoint its source. And we can't evaluate the success of our change, our realignment strategy, if we can't notice the resulting shifts in our lives. But the noticing can be deceptively complex as well.

Step One: Noticing

The first step of the alignment process, noticing, can be more challenging than it seems. Often, when we're out of alignment, we have a general sense of malaise, a feeling that things just aren't working the way they're "supposed to." And so pinpointing the source of our misalignment can be a challenge.

Not only that, but since alignment is rooted in honoring our most important wants (including living our values) while also meeting our deep human needs, we can bring a lot of our own baggage to the realignment process. Basically, in addition to the fact that we may not be very good at noticing subtle shifts in our lives, we might be substituting other things that don't take us to the root of the problem. We might say that work is the problem, for example, but not realize that the work challenges would be more manageable if our relationship with our partner was based in better communication strategies. The human experience is basically a story, and we can be good at false narratives, which makes it difficult to see ourselves and our lives clearly. This is normal and adorably human. Luckily, there are a few ways we can learn to get out of our own way to get better at noticing.

First, we can invite an outside perspective. Marta, one of my Montessori mentors, regularly insisted that everyone whose work impacted others needs some "supervision." She didn't care if it was a therapist, a rabbi, a life coach, a priest, or a social worker. But she maintained that it was absolutely critical for any of us whose work impacted human lives to have an outside perspective to help us with our noticing, so that we didn't inadvertently work out our own "stuff" on other people. For you, this person should be someone who is outside of your daily life, with whom you can be honest and who can support you in moving towards the life you want while also helping you to recognize any tendencies that don't serve your alignment. It's important to be clear that this kind of relationship is different from one you might have with a partner, family member, or close friend, for the same reason that therapists won't work with folks with whom they have natural connections already.

In my life, this outside perspective has been critical for the moments of realigning. It gave me a dedicated hour in my schedule and a safe space to consider my life, whether I was meeting weekly or monthly or something in between. In addition, if I already knew that I was out of alignment or heading that way, it was a place to work through what wasn't working and why. And this space also offered me some help with goal setting, to figure out whether the goals I was thinking would be helpful were likely to lead to the outcomes I wanted. And finally, the relationship offered me accountability in knowing that my coach will check in with me again.

I do recommend this kind of relationship to everyone, though I know that accessibility can be a challenge. Still, if you don't already have this person in your life, please visit my website (katiekellerwood.com), where you'll find resources that offer advice on how to find such a person and how to determine a good fit. The relationship can only help you improve your own noticing and alignment process if you can feel secure enough in the relationship to share freely, and if they understand and can support the alignment process.

That's not to say that our most trusted friends, family members, or partners can't provide any useful support here. They can! My most important people have also been the ones to hold up a mirror to my life, helping me to consider what is healthy for my life's alignment (though I never loved getting "the talk"). But because our most important relationships are both give and take, a trained coach, counselor, or therapist can have a more objective opinion, and can help us tune into our own needs and wants... our own deepest noticings.

While an outside perspective can be invaluable, the second way that we can greatly enhance our ability to tune into ourselves and our alignment is through personal practices. You've likely encountered them before, but perhaps you've not considered their utility in this way.

Mindfulness, sometimes called meditation, is one such practice. As defined by Jon Kabat-Zinn, mindfulness is "paying attention in a particular way: on purpose, in the present moment, and nonjudgmentally." It's this "nonjudgmental" piece of mindfulness that I want to call attention to now.

While I believe that quiet moments of reflection and meditation are useful for humans of all faith backgrounds, this kind of noticing, where judgment is suspended for a bit, is particularly helpful to the process of aligning. Mindfulness has become increasingly trendy in recent years, but it's rooted in an ancient practice. Throughout human history, religious leaders and sages have dedicated and protected time for quiet reflection. So whether you call it meditation, prayer, quiet time, or deep thinking, whether you involve writing or simply try to quiet your mind, whether you attach movement or strive for stillness, time spent in reflection can have profound effects. All are valuable, but if this kind of reflective time is new or even scary and uncomfortable, often one approach will be the most natural entry point. *If* you find that you are not able to engage in any of these approaches without a trauma response emerging, it is critical that you do begin work with a professional to help you find a way to attune to yourself safely.

A third way we can improve our noticing is when we practice being a friend and caretaker to ourselves. If you've ever taken care of a small child, you know that it's a job that requires patience and love. Humans are among the most helpless of mammals when they are born, and they are slower to develop when compared to many other species. Infants and small children need help with the most basic of human needs: food, clothing, protection. They are not yet capable of self-care. As we grow, we acquire more skills and become increasingly independent. As we move into adulthood, we learn to take responsibility for more of our own caretaking.

But we often lose sight of something along the way. We may be charged with our own caretaking, but we often aren't as kind or as gentle with ourselves as we might be with a small child. The way we speak to and about ourselves, and especially inside our own minds, matters more than we often realize. Negative self-talk is rarely conducive to living an aligned life, because it doesn't allow us to accurately notice our current life situations. There's simply too much judgment!

One strategy for remembering how to be a friend and caretaker to ourselves is remembering to think of ourselves as still carrying within us the precious children we once were. Author and activist Glennon Doyle has written and spoken about keeping a picture of herself as a small child on her dresser as a touchstone of who she really is, and as a reminder to treat herself the same way she would treat a precious child. In addition to reminding herself of who she was before absorbing too many messages of the world, it also reminded her that if she wouldn't speak to the child in the picture a certain way, she didn't want to speak to herself in her head that way. Keeping childhood pictures around is a brilliant visual reminder of who we truly are: a beloved and essential member of the human community.

As we learn to befriend ourselves, we may need to start with making sure our most basic needs are met. Givers can often "forget" to attend to themselves, with even the most basic requirements. You'll recall that physiological needs are the first tier on Maslow's hierarchy, and they need to be satisfied before we can attend to any of our other needs. One practice we can use to help us start noticing and tuning into our needs is to check in with ourselves at a regular interval. We might ask things like: Do I need to drink some water? Go to the bathroom? Eat something? Did I allow for adequate sleep last night, and can I make a plan to allow for adequate sleep tonight? Do I need to move my body more? Do I need to allow my body time to rest?

We can then move into meeting other needs, asking things like: How can I connect with a loved one today? What can I thank myself for? What can I celebrate?

Building a noticing habit takes time and intention, and by building the habit, you're already implementing an important change to support the healthy alignment of your life (more on supporting changes you want to make in your life in Chapter 8). Once your noticing habit has revealed a misalignment, the alignment process becomes a thinking tool to guide your next steps.

CHAPTER 4 SECOND PERIOD: THE PRACTICE

Writing Activity

An Olympian knows that maximum performance requires periods of maximum rest and recovery away from the arena, because we are whole people, so we have to take care of our whole selves. On a scale of 1 to 10, what would you rate your current ability to take care of your needs for:

- Nutrition
- Exercise
- Sleep
- Friendship
- Love
- Spiritual renewal (this may be religious for you, or you might think of it from a secular perspective as "nurturing your own spirit")
- Emotional and psychological well-being

If you're someone who regularly has trouble taking care of your most basic needs, I recommend that you use a sticky note, one that fits on the back of your phone, ID badge, or other item you keep with you all day, to keep track of check-in questions, like:

1. Water tally _____
2. Movement tally _____
3. Fuel tally _____
4. Connections today _____

And maybe a reminder and plan for adequate rest. But play with it! What do *you* most need to practice noticing? Try it for two weeks and see if you notice any shifts.

And if you're someone who can be challenged to remember to speak kindly to yourself, try journaling about your daily wins for two weeks. I love a tiny notebook, something easy to keep by the bed. (Making notes digitally just isn't the same!) These are the things you are thanking yourself for, and they can be as simple or complex as the day allows. Give it just one minute but really feel the gratitude. Sometimes, getting out the door on time, taking a shower, making sure everybody eats, letting someone know you care about them, or getting a load of laundry done are the wins of the day. Don't discount them! And if it helps, feel free to also pull out a childhood picture of yourself for your journal.

Reflection Questions
- Looking at your answers in the writing activity, does anything stand out as needing to be reprioritized in your life mosaic? What would it take to make just one change this week?

- Which strategies for building a noticing habit are present in your life already: inviting an outside perspective (a therapist, coach, spiritual leader, or mentor), cultivating a regular mindfulness or quiet reflection practice, or intentionally taking on the role of caretaker to yourself (caring for yourself the way that you might care for a small child)?

- Which of the above strategies might be helpful to add in?

- Are there other strategies that (could or do) help you to tune in and really notice the ebb and flow of your life?

CHAPTER 4 THIRD PERIOD: THE APPLICATION

Notice

Commit to building your noticing habit.

That's it, and while simple, it might not be easy. Building a habit takes practice! You might find the writing or journaling activities described in the second period practice helpful, but you might also decide to seek out that outside perspective, schedule regular time for quiet reflection, take a mindfulness class, or something else that came to you in your reflections above.

Whatever you decide, share this commitment with your valued other, and see if they can support you as you work to build this critical habit. As we build our capacity to notice, we'll be quicker to recognize sources of misalignment, and therefore quicker to adjust. But the noticing is essential; the alignment process requires our ability to accurately tune into our own lives.

5

Finding Alignment, Part II: Addressing Misalignment

I COULDN'T BELIEVE IT when I heard that an acquaintance of mine, Alan, had quit his job. He had been an integral part of a small law firm for several years where a friend of mine worked. Alan knew, and mostly really liked, all the clients. When I met him, Alan had told me that the best part of his job was feeling that he was making a difference in helping to serve clients and their legal needs. And by all accounts, he was great at his job. It came with some big responsibilities, but Alan was incredibly thorough, and he had a perfect personality for interacting with clients in a way that reaffirmed their trust in the firm as a whole.

From the outside, his job had seemed to offer him everything. He felt satisfaction in the work, he said that he liked his boss, and he was well compensated. In fact, my friend shared with me that Alan was paid probably 20 percent more than others with similar roles at other firms, and about double what most cost-of-living indices said a family needed to "live comfortably" in his city. His hours were regular, a predictable nine-to-five, and there was a flexible remote-work policy, so Alan spent about half of his time working from home. Because it was a small firm, everyone enjoyed an unlimited vacation policy, pitching in to cover when others were out. Planned time off went on the team calendar a few months ahead of time, but if Alan ever needed to leave early or come late to support his family, that was generally fine, too. Alan wasn't expected to take calls, check email, or otherwise work outside of business hours, with the exception of a few special events held by the firm.

To be honest, I had been more than a little envious of Alan! I didn't want to do his work, of course, but he seemed like he was living the dream, at least workwise! Alan had a job that mattered to him, where he felt he could make a difference, and where he was respected, trusted, and supported. Most teachers I knew would never make Alan's salary. Most nurses I knew would never have the kind of flexibility Alan had. And everyone I know wants the kind of trust from their supervisors that Alan enjoyed.

But clearly all of this wasn't enough. Alan asked for a private meeting with his boss one day and indicated that, for the first time, he was thinking of leaving the firm. He shared his specific concerns, and they had several "heart to heart" conversations to brainstorm a way forward. Alan's boss was ready to try pretty much anything. But when suggestion after suggestion that she made was shot down, Alan's boss wondered if some burnout might also be at play. There were definitely some things going on at home, but Alan had been vague about the details. Alan and his boss decided that he would take some time off to really think things over and decide on the needs and direction of his life. But Alan came back at the end of this mini-sabbatical and gave his notice, ending his time at the firm that everyone had thought would last decades.

Alan was where many of us have been at different points in our lives: feeling that something about his work wasn't working. It was easy to blame something like discomfort with the way the firm was growing, but that didn't seem to be Alan's entire story. (If that had been the only issue, surely he and his boss could have found a solution.) Even Alan's job flexibility and extended time off hadn't made a difference.

What I wish I could have shared with Alan is this: the path to alignment isn't found by simply deciding to stay or to leave a job or career, though those considerations are important. Noticing that there's a problem, all on its own, also won't be enough to resolve the tension. We have to find a way to get clear on what the problem actually is, because if we are trying to solve the wrong problem, we're not going to find an elegant solution.

When I heard that Alan had left, I couldn't help but speculate a bit on what had gone wrong. I wondered if perhaps blaming work made for an easier change in Alan's life than working through other issues, which could have felt more daunting to him, or might have been more complex. And while I'll never know the full story, it struck me as more than a little heartbreaking to see someone who loved their work, and who was so good at it, choose to walk away.

So while this next part may seem simple, it's not easy. But my hope for all of us is that when we can learn to notice our misalignment, even a slight one, we can then also determine the real issues that are impacting our holistic alliance, so that we'll be equipped to make shifts well before the situation becomes dire. We need to be able to start implementing solutions well before we reach burnout, well before we can see no other option but the most drastic (and potentially wrong) one, as I suspected had been the case for Alan.

As I mentioned in the last chapter, the alignment process is best described as part habit, part thinking tool. Chapter 4 addressed the habit part: so that we can notice when our needs and most important wants aren't being honored. This chapter addresses the thinking tool: the questions we ask ourselves once we've noticed that we're out of alignment.

Step Two: Asking—Work or Nonwork?

Noticing is the first step of the alignment process. The second step, once we have noticed a misalignment, is to ask ourselves which pieces of our life mosaic most need our attention: work pieces, nonwork pieces, or perhaps both.

This is tricky, because we are whole humans, and our mosaic pieces are part of that whole, so often a challenge or a change to some pieces in our work-life alliance will impact the others.

When my sister Abby called me that October day when she was having "a little hard time" and wondering if it was time to quit her job, there was one other critical factor at play: timing. It was the fall of 2020, and her hospital, like all others, was still in the throes of a global pandemic, and no one knew how long it would last.

So I asked her to consider one important question. "Abbs," I told her, "your work has always been hard." She agreed. "And for sure the pandemic has made everything harder for hospital workers. But do you think you'd be feeling this way if the other parts of your life hadn't also been interrupted by the pandemic? If you were able to see your friends, your family?

Would it be this same amount of hard if you could still go to the gym the way you used to?" I knew that Abby's life, like all of ours, had changed dramatically during the pandemic lockdown. She still went to work, but because she worked oncology, and her patients had very compromised immune systems, she was extra vigilant about avoiding any COVID exposures outside of her work. She hadn't seen anyone outside of her neighbors, not even her immediate family, in months. Her gym had closed. She had even had to say goodbye to her best furry friend. Abby could see that the work, while more difficult, wasn't the only part of her life that had shifted.

We're whole humans, living our whole lives, so our work isn't separate from the rest of our lives. This is why our deep noticing habits have to come first. Without them, we might still have a feeling of misalignment, but if we jump to step two without spending time tuned into our deepest needs and wants, we can easily misdiagnose the problems we're facing. Without time spent paying attention to our whole lives, an annoying colleague might seem to be making our work life untenable. And for sure, we may need some good boundaries or to renegotiate aspects of our work life (more on that in Chapter 7). But if we're more irritable than normal because we're chronically sleep deprived, getting away from a colleague may not solve our problems.

Step Three: Asking—Internal or External Shift?

When we think we've identified the primary source of our healthy alliance breakdown, the third step of the alignment process is to determine whether an internal shift or an external shift (or again both) is required.

An internal shift is a change that I can make myself; I don't need the participation of anyone else. Though I say "internal," the shift may or may not be observable to others. Less observable internal shifts could include learning to change my attitude, thought patterns, or self-talk. More observable internal shifts could include learning a new skill, setting a new boundary, implementing a new habit, or otherwise starting to organize aspects of my life differently. This book has a number of suggestions for possible internal shifts, both in this and in later chapters. And the beautiful thing about personal development (more on that in Chapter 6) is that it can help us grow our capacity, so we can have even more space for our most beautiful and important life mosaic pieces.

But not *everything* is within our control. Sometimes we need external shifts, where other people participate in some way, to happen as well. Some of these external shifts are likely quite possible without a major overhaul of our environment, as when we seek to outsource or delegate tasks, when we renegotiate our wants and needs with others, or we seek to strengthen our network of supportive relationships. We don't always need a new job, new city, new puppy, or a new partner. And thank goodness, because constantly making major changes like that sounds exhausting! Very often, we can advocate for the changes we need and want within our current environments, tweaking them so that they better support our own thriving, and likely the thriving of others as well.

I'll say it again: our advocacy often enhances not only our own thriving but the thriving of others as well. You're not being "difficult" when you advocate for your own needs and deepest desires. One of my favorite quotes from Senator Paul Wellstone (as shared with me by my Montessori mentor Marta) is "We all do better when we all do better." It's simple, but profound. It's why if you have a question in a seminar, you should ask, because chances are someone else was wondering the same thing. When you advocate to make a workplace safer or more inclusive, it is safer and more inclusive for everyone. And when you are a model of how to lovingly advocate for your own needs, you not only give the same permission to others, but you also become a model for how to live an aligned life, a life of not settling for or accepting less than you need and deserve. Your alignment matters, both for your own life and for the many lives you touch. (More on that idea in the final chapter!)

Internal and external shifts can apply equally to both our work and our nonwork pieces of our life's alliance. For example, I can change how I think about and react to a supervisor just as much as I can change how I think about and react to my partner. Similarly, I may need to negotiate certain things with my partner (like household responsibilities) or with my supervisor (like taking on more/less/different responsibilities). Both work and nonwork pieces can require internal and/or external shifts to support a healthy alliance.

Step Four: Implementing

The fourth step of the alignment process is simple, though not necessarily easy. When we've moved through the thinking tool, asking ourselves the necessary questions about what pieces of our life mosaic to address and how, we implement our changes, and then go back to paying attention. Of course, implementation can be challenging: it's not easy to establish new habits, advocate for ourselves, or uphold healthy boundaries. We may need to learn new things, ask for support, and challenge ourselves to be brave. And the second half of this book will offer some practical supports for different alignment challenges. But nevertheless, after we decide on the shifts to make, we move to implementation. And with each implementation, we're immediately back to step one, our noticing habit. We come back to ourselves, attuning and tending to the needs and wants of our life mosaic like a garden, ever growing, ever changing. This is why the alignment process can never be linear; we'll always come back to our noticing habit. We'll always come home to ourselves.

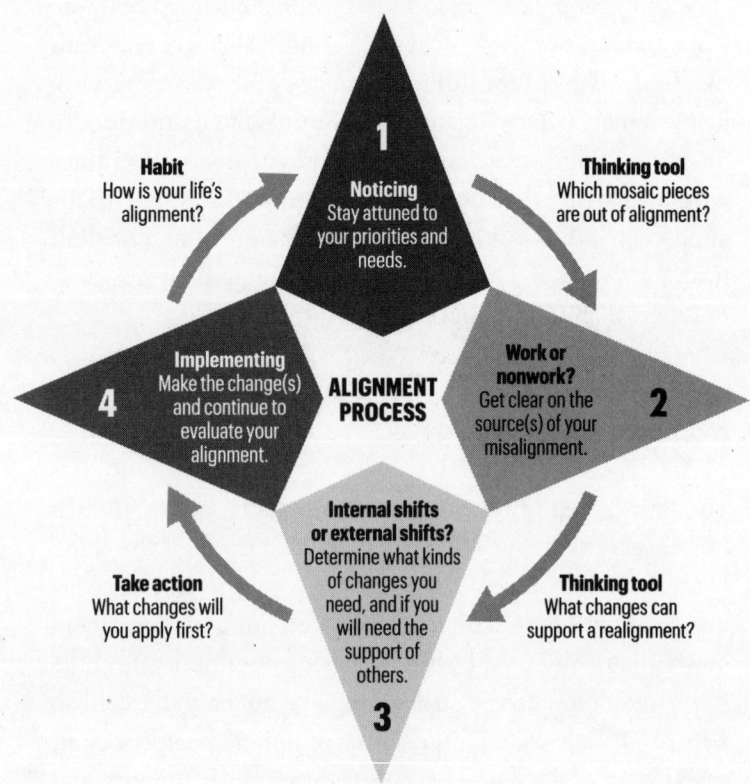

Bored Overwhelm

As we learn to return to ourselves again and again, we may notice a specific alignment challenge creep in from time to time: feeling less meaning (than we want to) in our various mosaic pieces. Of course, not all our responsibilities are going to feel meaningful all the time. But there can be a tipping point in noticing less meaning in our work that often impacts our whole mosaic.

Maybe it's happened to you already: Have you experienced the paradox of feeling both completely overwhelmed by the work on your plate, but bored with it all at the same time? Bored overwhelm is a specific alignment challenge, one that we can learn to notice and address. Bored overwhelm isn't exclusively a work problem, though; it can show up in the nonwork pieces of our mosaic, too—anytime that we have a lot on our plate, but we're feeling less connected to the meaning behind it.

Bored overwhelm is a terrible feeling: your to-do list is a million miles long, you're waking up in the middle of the night with that one more thing you *almost* forgot about, but even though you have easily ten, twenty, or even more things that you could list that you absolutely *must* take care of this week, absolutely none of them calls to you right now. Not one. You just don't want to.

You can still see why the work is important: you know that the contributions you make to these things in the long term do help. And you do want your students to have thoughtful feedback to help them improve, your patients to have a team of hospital caregivers who are able to recognize domestic violence, and the accreditation reports to be accurate. Oh, and you don't want your car insurance to get canceled, or to run out of diapers, or to miss the only dermatologist appointment available for the next 937 days, either.

But there's no meaning to the work.

I've wrestled with this kind of bored overwhelm at different periods throughout my career; I don't think I've ever had a job where it didn't pop up at least sometimes. In my early years of teaching, I would carry around student work that needed my review. It was literally my burden to bear until it got done, and the burden ranged from a Friday quiz (two hundred total pages for all my sections) to a class's worth of composition notebooks in one of those thirteen-inch cube storage bins with handles. (Target thinks these are for storing your items artfully on open shelving, but they are really for teachers to transport student work too unwieldy for a shoulder bag.) "How was your weekend?" a colleague would ask. "Oh, I gave my student journals a tour of the state, never opening one of them. But thanks for asking!"

And the problem with bored overwhelm is that it impacts your work in other ways. For me, it's usually one of two things: You know the things you need to do, so you don't make progress on anything, because if you're going to get some work done it needs to be on that list! This is the particularly soul-crushing part of bored overwhelm: the list is so long, so seemingly unmanageable, that you don't do anything at all. The resistance to the work is so strong, but you're *always* aware of the long list of tasks that you're not making progress on. You know the to-do list isn't going anywhere.

Or the opposite: I need to do all the little things before I can do the important thing. Writing can be like that for me. For a long time (okay, still sometimes) I deluded myself that I can't write unless every email is answered, every dish is washed and put away, every room relatively tidy. I couldn't write in clutter, mental or physical, so I spent untold amounts of time trying to clear all the clutter. Even in graduate school, I once remarked to a friend that nothing made me more productive than having a big paper due: I'd clean the whole house, launder all the stuff that you only get to sporadically, and reorganize every closet before I sat down to write. Writer and leadership speaker Jon Acuff calls this a hiding place, which I like much better than the conventional label of procrastination, because the reasons for my flurries of activity were more complex than simple avoidance.

Bored overwhelm is more likely to pop up anytime we're faced with a lot of administrative pieces, long-term projects, or items that are important but not necessarily time-bound or urgent. And some of us have a lot of this kind of work in our roles. But even the most action-oriented, mission-driven jobs, like first responders, still have paperwork. I used to think that paramedics spent all their time in an ambulance responding to emergencies, that their work was all action, all immediate. But when I interviewed a paramedic, her stories were illuminating. Because yes, the calls come in, and that work is immediate. But there was also a lot of time with their reports (both from the calls and other kinds of long-term reporting), their checklists, their cleaning and restocking protocols, and their continued training.

Floor nurses may spend most of the shift with the immediate work of attending to patient needs, but they also still have mandatory training and committee work. Now, bored overwhelm is less likely when administrative tasks have to happen within a particular time frame. We *think* we want flexibility and options to do our work whenever and wherever we like, but fewer choices can be better when we're facing work that has to get done but we don't particularly want to do it. Floor nurses have to give report at the end of the shift; there's no "I'll get to that tomorrow," so for floor nurses, charting and giving report are less likely to contribute to bored overwhelm. In fact, the more we can keep our work to this time and this place, not giving ourselves the option of "a hiding place," the less opportunity bored overwhelm has to creep in.

Here are four strategies that work for me when the bored overwhelm is temporary, when I'm not at the point of considering quitting. (And usually, these strategies can keep me from getting to that feeling!)

1. **Schedule the tasks.** It can be difficult to estimate how long things are actually going to take, but do your best, remembering also Parkinson's law: work expands or contracts to fill the amount of time available. So give the task or project the time you think it needs on your calendar. If I have a chunk of time set aside for working on a project, if I know it's on my calendar, I can often set down the burden of that to-do item. But I have to keep my word to myself. I have to be like the floor nurse giving report: there can't be any wiggle room. When that time rolls around on the calendar, I have to give it my whole attention for the entire thirty minutes. I might have to monitor my progress and hurry to keep the task to the time frame allotted.

2. **Find accountability.** Tell someone when you're going to do the work and, ideally, have them with or near you when you do it, even if that's virtually. (I love to meet for Zoom writing sessions with other authors!) This is best when you can build on the scheduling strategy above: you set the time to work on the thing, and you have someone else (virtually or in person) who knows what you're working on

and who also will know if you *don't* do the thing. Report your progress.

3 **Snowball your to-do list.** Pick the easiest win, the thing you can most quickly cross of the to-do list, and then do one more. Inertia is strong, but so is forward momentum. Find a way to build some momentum, and then just keep it going.

4 **Celebrate the wins.** When you've been stuck in bored overwhelm, the only way through it is to start taking even tiny steps of action, because these can lead to bigger steps. But not if you don't feel like they count. If the voice in your head discounts the small progress, it's not going to inspire bigger progress. So we have to celebrate the small wins, appreciating the work that we did, even when we didn't feel like it, and reminding ourselves of how that work really does make a difference in the grand scheme of things. For example, I know that accreditation reports are important to keep our accreditation, and without that, our organization would be significantly less able to do our important work impacting lives. And yet, the annual reports and substantive change processes can fill me with dread. And so, not only do I call on other team members for support and accountability, but we also celebrate each tiny step, which keeps us moving. When we reach the finish line, when the reports are submitted, we treat ourselves by going out for lunch together!

But sometimes bored overwhelm is the precursor to burnout. This is more serious, because you can still see why the work matters, and it's not so simple as you just "need a new challenge," because more to-dos on your plate are only going to add to the soul-crushing weight you already feel. In that case, you need a change, because something about the meaningful work isn't meaningful for you anymore. So, if you're not ready to leave, it's time to engage your network. What can come off your plate? What roles could you switch with someone? Where could you get support? And by the way, this role-switching and support can come in the nonwork parts of your life, too. In stressful work times, my partner and I radically reorganize our normal household contributions.

The point here is to reestablish meaning in the various demands of our mosaic pieces. We're not going to find it 100 percent of the time, but there's a dissatisfaction tipping point—if we start to feel that the majority of our work tasks are no longer meaningful, we're going to be dissatisfied. I think it's reasonable to extrapolate that to our whole life mosaic; if the majority of our time is spent on items that don't feel remotely important or meaningful, then we're in need of some alignment shifts.

We may also need to look to our mosaic more holistically. Montessori's ideas of interleaving, resting from one kind of work with another, can be useful. Head, hands, heart work are all important. If your work is all in your head, how can you get into your body? Walking, yoga, and (more recently) basket weaving have been amazing for me. If your body is weary from physical work, is there a more abstract problem you could puzzle over? And if your heart needs a reconnection, where can you go to reconnect to your why? While I spend a lot of my time with more abstract work, I love visiting teachers in their classrooms. These visits remind me of who our training program really serves: the emergent adults of our species. Seeing these young people, their brilliance and creativity, their commitment to a better world, never fails to fill my heart and inspire me. What might you need to spend time working on or noticing to reconnect to the meaning in your pieces of the work puzzle?

Perfection Is a Fantasy

Remember, living a life of alignment isn't about being perfect. It's about continually coming home to yourself and your life. It's about noticing if you are living your values and being a good caretaker for yourself. It's about checking in and seeing how well your work and your nonwork are supporting each other, and if your wants and needs are being met. It's about seeing if changes are needed within yourself or in your environment. And then it's about making these changes and monitoring their outcomes.

The correct positions of work and nonwork in your life will change over time, but no matter how your mosaic shifts, it can be beautifully aligned at any stage. In the next part of the book, we'll look at a process and a system to continually return to yourself, allowing you to honor the alliance in support of your one tiny and treasured life.

CHAPTER 5 SECOND PERIOD: THE PRACTICE

This chapter's follow-up work is differentiated. The practice options (second period) are the same, but the application (third period) is not. If you have noticed that you are out of alignment, I've offered some supports to help you use the thinking tools explored in this chapter to move through the alignment process.

Writing Activity

To play with the thinking tool of recognizing work pieces from nonwork pieces:

- List some of the challenges you're feeling from your work pieces.

- List some of the benefits you're feeling from your work pieces.

- List some of the supports you're receiving from your nonwork pieces.

- List some of the supports you wish you were receiving from your nonwork pieces.

Reflection Questions

- Have you had the experience of thinking the source of your problems was one thing (person, situation) but found later that there were other factors at play as well? How did you figure that out? How might your noticing practices help with these kinds of false narratives?

- Have you felt bored overwhelm in your life? What circumstances seem to prompt this for you? What are your typical responses? What might you try next time this pops up for you?

- Where in your mosaic can you practice interleaving, resting from one type of work with another? If your work is mostly in your head, how can you get into your body? If your work is often physical, can you make time for some more abstract problem-solving?

- For all work pieces, are you able to see connections to your purpose work or your paycheck work? Or are there mosaic pieces that feel less meaningful to you?

CHAPTER 5 THIRD PERIOD: THE APPLICATION

Completing the Alignment Process

If you are currently feeling that your work and nonwork are in a supportive alliance, promoting a healthy life alignment (or at least nothing stands out as needing to be addressed), then there's no application (third period) of this content yet. My recommendation for you is that you keep practicing your noticing! Return to this chapter's follow-up work when you are next facing a misalignment. Change is inevitable, so we will be aligning and realigning for the rest of our tiny and treasured lives.

If you *are* feeling out of alignment, it's time to apply (actually, move through) the rest of the steps of the alignment process. To support your first application here, I've broken things down even further from the two essential questions, which are highlighted in bold.

1 From your lists in the writing activity above, what pieces stand out as potentially driving your current misalignment? List one or two items. **Are they work pieces, nonwork pieces, or both?**

As another way to discern here, take a minute to think about what it would be like if these pieces were instead contributing to your life's healthy alliance. How would your life be different? Do you still feel confident that these are the pieces you want to address?

2. **Can these pieces be brought back into alignment with purely internal shifts (which you can do yourself) or will they require external shifts (which includes some collaboration from others)?** Can you list items in both categories? For example, you might want to both change a habit and meet with your team to discuss a redistribution of current caseload responsibilities. List as many possibilities you can think of.

Choose one or two shifts that you think will make the biggest difference for your life's alignment. Think about how long you need to try (or are willing to give) for this new approach to be effective.

3. Implement your changes and return to your noticing practices.

PART 2

SUPPORTING A HEALTHY ALLIANCE

Aligning and Realigning

6

Expanding Your Mosaic: Montessori for Adult Development

WHEN I WAS TEACHING, it was common in our Montessori middle school program for graduates to return if they had a day off from high school, choosing to spend their day off back in our community, reconnecting with friends and teachers. (This in itself was remarkable to me, because the last place I wanted to go after moving on was *back* to my middle school.) Anya, who had been a student at our Montessori school for many years, decided to join us for a typical day, and the other students were eager to hear *everything* about high school life. Anya jumped into the activities of the day, participating in our poetry discussion and writer's workshop, and kindly answered all the questions that the middle schoolers had about her life in high school.

But I will never forget what she shared with me in a more private moment at the end of the day. In describing her move to this much larger high school, she talked about making friends. She told me that when she first arrived, she was quick to join a fall sport. This wasn't a surprise; Anya had always been athletic, and she had participated in a number of club sports throughout the time that I knew her. Joining the team was helpful for providing her with a ready-made network, since she didn't know anyone else at the school when classes began. But she told me that she soon realized, with some of her team time, that several members of this group "didn't quite share her values," but that she still wanted an authentic community. So Anya decided that, while remaining friendly with everyone and working hard as a team throughout the season, she would also set out to make a new group of friends.

I was floored.

Here was a fourteen-year-old with enough sense of self to realize that she didn't want to spend her weekends with the party set, but neither did she need to bad-mouth or completely disassociate from them. Instead, she could simply notice and articulate the difference in values, confident in her own.

I mean, I've known plenty of grown adults who would like to have the kind of self-awareness and confidence that Anya showed. It's one thing to be able to make a hard choice to "do the right thing," which we also want for our young people. But Anya went beyond black-and-white, right-or-wrong thinking. She was able to name her own values and make her life choices accordingly, *without* denigrating the choices of others. That's another level! I still think of Anya, and all the Montessori students that I taught, frequently. They taught me so many lessons; they were the embodiment of the Montessori ideas of respect for self and for others, of using your gifts and talents to make the world a better place. I was able to observe human and adolescent development close-up, to see them truly becoming themselves. And what I saw most of all was a healthy container for a young person's most important work: self-construction. And in my work with teachers over the last decade-plus, I've seen that the work of self-construction continues, especially when the environment is conducive for growth. The best news? I am convinced that we can *all* create these kinds of containers for ourselves.

In the same way that Montessori classrooms aim to support the healthy development of children and adolescents, a Montessori approach can support our self-construction as adults, equipping us to navigate the challenges of our increasingly complex world. This not only helps us solve problems with increased skill when we are out of alignment, it also helps us grow our life mosaics all together, creating even more space for the pieces that matter to us.

Developmental Experiences: Growing Our Mosaics

Maria Montessori believed in education as a vehicle for the creation of a better world. Specifically, she believed that if each child and adolescent could be allowed to develop on their own timetable into the adult they were meant to be, understanding their own unique gifts and how those gifts can contribute to and function in relationship with others, it would lead to a more peaceful and just world. Montessori classrooms, then, are designed to function as a developmental container for students, "developmental" meaning that they aid in human development, in capacity-building. Each item in a Montessori classroom has a particular purpose and is designed with the students (of a particular age span) in mind, so that even the youngest students can navigate the classroom as independently as possible, growing their capacities and sense of self-efficacy. "Help me to do it alone" is the child's cry, according to Montessori.

And not only do these Montessori classrooms have lessons to teach us about how we might reimagine our own work, but the Montessori approach also has important implications and applications for our own adult development. Dr. Montessori addressed adult development in relation to her theories about what is required to be a Montessori teacher (she believed that the effective Montessori teacher had to be "transformed," which required a realization of their own full potential and ability for personal growth), and she also had some writings on parenting.

But as I've stated, I don't think that Montessori's ideas have to be limited to the tiny percentage of human students who are able to attend Montessori schools, though I'm encouraged that Montessori schools, and especially public Montessori schools, are growing worldwide. And I don't think you have to attend Montessori teacher training to learn to apply some of these ideas to your own life. Because I've seen over the last fifteen-plus years that utilizing Montessori approaches in our adult work and life can support holistic adult development, thereby increasing our capacity to work and live with greater joy, self-confidence, and purpose in an ever-changing world.

Ellie Drago-Severson, a Columbia University professor and an expert in adult learning and development, regularly speaks to this idea of living in an increasingly complex world. It's not enough to have informational knowledge, the kind that is increasingly available via the tiny computers we carry around and even wear. Informational knowledge is most useful when the challenges we face have a known solution, like a broken refrigerator. Those are technical challenges. There's an answer to that repair, and someone, somewhere, can tell you what it is. But we also face adaptive challenges. These are challenges that do not have an already-known solution. There are big ones, like climate change, and day-to-day ones, like how best to get along with a colleague you find difficult. No one can tell you what the exact answer is; it doesn't already exist. Learning to navigate life's inevitable changes, like chronic illness, career transitions, marriage, divorce, or raising children, all present adaptive challenges. There's no instruction manual for any of these things.

And with the increasing complexity of our world, we all face more and more adaptive challenges. So informational learning isn't enough. To meet adaptive challenges, we need to increase our capacity to manage our continuously transforming lives, which requires developmental experiences leading to transformational learning. Drago-Severson describes this difference as the kind of learning that "fills the vessel" (informational learning, which is still important) and the kind of learning that "changes the shape of the vessel" (transformational learning). It is this transformational learning, which comes only through developmental experiences, that increases our capacity, allowing us to grow our life mosaic.

To make this a bit more concrete, compare your life and adult responsibilities now to when you first entered the workforce. Odds are, you have some important mosaic pieces now that did not exist then. And you've built the corresponding capacity to manage this increased complexity over time. Most Americans enter the workforce in a full-time role between eighteen and twenty-five years of age. But the average age of marriage, children, and full financial independence is often later. Maintaining a household, a partner relationship, or a family represent significant pieces of our life's mosaic, and these are skills that we learn over time, building our capacity to manage the increased complexity of our lives. In our work as well, we build capacity over time through developmental experiences. Things that were scary or difficult in the early parts of our career become easier, more automatic, allowing us to grow in new ways. This is how leadership skills are honed.

I remember when Abby was a new nurse in her first weeks of independent practice at the hospital. She had earned high marks in all her nursing classes, done very well on the NCLEX-RN exam, and earned praise from her preceptor and supervisors at the hospital. Everyone agreed she was ready and well prepared for independent nursing. And yet, she was *terr-i-fied*. The stakes were high, literally life and death for some of her work. And oncology floor nursing, managing care for a set of patients over a twelve-hour (or let's face it, fourteen-hour) shift provided an endless stream of things to keep track of, decisions to make, and unknown situations to navigate. Abby also saw grief, suffering, and death on a regular basis as a young professional.

It got easier for Abby, as our work usually does, and she came to find great meaning, pride, and personal fulfillment in her work. It's true for most professions: the first year of teaching new content is much harder than the third year of teaching that content. But remembering how we got from there to here can also help us see that more is possible. As Harvard psychologist Daniel Gilbert explained in his TED Talk, "human beings are works in progress who mistakenly think they're finished." But we're not done! Human development can continue indefinitely, and these kinds of capacity-building containers, the learning situations that aid in our self-construction, enhance our healthy alignment. They can help us recognize and make changes when we are out of alignment, because we are more in touch with and confident about who we are, and they can literally help us grow our mosaics, creating even more space for pieces that matter to us, because we have developed new capacities.

To understand how and why a Montessori approach helps us with self-construction, the next section is going to cover a handful of theories regarding human development and motivation, two of which were mentioned briefly in Chapter 4: Abraham Maslow's hierarchy of needs and Richard Ryan and Edward Deci's self-determination theory. Why theory, in a practical book about finding alignment? Because when we understand what is required to support healthy human development, including our own, we have a clearer path for creating these kinds of containers for ourselves.

Creating Developmental Experiences: Human Motivation

Developmental psychologist Abraham Maslow proposed that human motivation is driven by a hierarchy of needs, and that as needs at the lower levels are satisfied (including the need for food, water, sleep, shelter), humans could turn their attention to the development of other areas, satisfying "higher" needs, like belonging. His highest level of need fulfillment, in the initial model, was termed "self-actualization," a term that even people who don't know Maslow may be familiar with. Essentially, a self-actualizing person, according to Maslow, was someone who was fulfilling their own human potential.

Montessori had similar goals for her educational method, writing that the ultimate goal regarding the education of older students (adolescents) was that they would experience what she called a "valorization of the personality." Put simply,

Montessori's idea of valorization was that through the developmental experiences of their education, a young person would enter the world of adult society feeling confident in their own self-worth and seeing themselves as having important contributions to make to the world.

Maslow described self-actualizing individuals as "people who have developed or are developing to the full stature of which they are capable." He also wrote that "Self-actualizing people are... involved in a cause outside their own skin, in something outside of themselves... something which fate has called them to somehow and which they work at and which they love, so that the work-joy dichotomy there disappears." It's easy to see from the quotes above some similarities between Maslow's self-actualization and Montessori's valorization, including a perspective of work that even the youngest Montessori students have embodied.

Maslow's ideas are not without critics, so while still significant, others have come along to refine and propose alternative theories of motivation. One such theory is self-determination theory (SDT), proposed by psychologists Richard Ryan and Edward Deci.

SDT proposes that human beings have three basic psychological needs that are essential for fostering both motivation and growth. They are the human need for autonomy, competence, and relatedness. Research on thriving (briefly discussed in Chapter 3) supports the idea that when we can create environments that support these three needs, human development and thriving can follow. Indeed, research by Ryan and Deci indicates that when these three needs are met, people are more likely to experience greater well-being and to perform at a higher level across various domains.

Autonomy refers to the need to feel in control of one's actions, to make decisions for oneself, and to choose behaviors aligned with personal values. In the Montessori classroom, students are given a great deal of choice around the work that they complete. While not everything is a choice, one hallmark of a Montessori classroom is that students choose what work to complete within their "work cycle" time. When it comes to our work as adults, feeling that we have some control and autonomy, that we get to make choices about our work, and that our work does not contradict our values, is also important.

Competence refers to the human need to feel effective, that we are capable of making a difference and achieving what we set out to do. It doesn't mean that we never experience failure. In fact, research would indicate that adopting a mastery orientation (where one is always seeking to improve skills and learn from failure) as opposed to a performance orientation (where one is focused on performance relative to others) can support feelings of competence. This is one reason that competition is de-emphasized in a Montessori classroom. If every human has unique talents, and no two humans develop exactly on the same timetable, then having students focused on comparing themselves to one another is not a helpful tool for learning and development. Competence in the workplace can be supported by providing a "just right" challenge level (challenging but achievable goals), receiving supportive and actionable feedback, and having regular opportunities for continuous learning and growth.

Finally, relatedness refers to the need to feel connected to others, experiencing a sense of belonging. Montessori classrooms are known for the social-emotional learning supports they offer. One of my Montessori mentors, Marta, regularly reminded us that we were trying to create in our classrooms a "high-functioning mini-society," where everyone was seen and valued for their contributions to the whole. In our work, we experience relatedness when we feel that we have supportive colleagues, when we have a sense of a shared mission in doing work that matters to us, and when we feel that everyone's perspective matters.

So where does all that lead us? Ellie Drago-Severson posits that adults need developmental learning containers, places where we can grow our capacity to manage complexity, adapt to challenges, make decisions, and think and relate to others more flexibly. Her work indicates that for an experience to be developmental (that is, for an experience or environment to help us grow in our capacities), it will entail some mixture (or ideally all) of the following: a "supportive challenge" (where someone is stretched just beyond current capacities, but also supported to be able to meet the challenge), opportunities for reflection, collaboration with others (including teamwork and mentoring), and encouragement of autonomy. A Montessori classroom embodies all these principles as well. So since most of us can't, at this point in our lives, spend significant time in a Montessori classroom, the question becomes, what can we do to create more Montessori-like developmental containers for ourselves, in our work and lives?

Creating a Montessori Container in Our Work and Lives

In Chapter 2, I presented ten things Montessori classrooms can teach us about work and a discussion of what it could look like to implement those things in our lives. Building on those lessons, and now also the theories above, here's what the creation of a Montessori-like developmental container could offer.

First, this kind of container will be a place where we can engage as a whole person. We will be able to bring all of who we are—intellectually, emotionally, spiritually, socially, and even physically—as humans with bodies. We won't be asked to compartmentalize ourselves or our lives. We'll be encouraged to engage in our work with all parts of our intersecting identities, not feeling a need to hide important parts of ourselves to fit a certain narrative. We'll bring our talents, passions, and joys, and we'll be able to be honest about reservations, fears, hurt, or sorrow.

We bring all of who we are to this place, because it is precisely our unique brand of magic that gives us a unique role to fill in the universe. We can't fulfill our purpose work by being anything less than our fullest selves. That also means that we have a responsibility to spend time with who we are, and not just what we do, in the world. Our efficacy in the world requires that we continue to find or create capacity-building containers for our ongoing self-construction and development.

Second, this kind of container will provide work that feels meaningful, respected, and has a just-right challenge level. We will reflect on our work and ourselves, giving and receiving feedback. We'll be provided with high expectations, opportunities to stretch just beyond our current comfort zones, but we'll have high support as we strive for these new accomplishments. We'll have teams and mentors that see and support our full humanity. We'll have choices and autonomy in our work. And even when we miss the mark, work-product created with earnest efforts is still treated with respect, as evidence of human life-force energy.

I believe our places of work, whether we'd call it our paycheck work, purpose work, or both, can be developmental containers that enhance our whole lives. Maybe you've happened upon such a place already, or you see elements in your workplace that are supportive of human development. But if you see room for improvement, I also believe that we can lead from wherever we are to create better developmental environments in our current settings. If you hold a leadership position in an organization, you might have a special responsibility to consider whether your organization's culture supports this kind of developmental container. But even if you hold no formal title, you can still talk about, advocate for, and choose to live out this kind of Montessori approach. You can choose or advocate for meaningful work, you can spend time in reflection, you can model appreciation for the work product of those around you. You can help create this kind of container, for yourself and for others.

CHAPTER 6 SECOND PERIOD: THE PRACTICE

Writing Activity

Review the last section of this chapter and the description of a Montessori-like developmental container for our work and lives. Which of these elements are present for you today? Which elements would you like to see improved?

Reflection Questions

- Where does your work provide you with feelings of autonomy, competence, and relatedness? Where do you see room for growth in these areas?

- Over the years, how has your work contributed to new capacities for you as a person? What can you do now that was at least daunting, if not hard or impossible, at earlier stages of your adult development?

- What new capacities would you like to continue to build? And what would your life be like if your mosaic continued to grow (as a result of these new capacities) so that you created more space for the pieces that matter to you?

- Drago-Severson posits that we need supportive challenge, opportunities for reflection, collaboration with others, and encouragement of autonomy for a container to be "developmental." Which of these are present in your work environment today? Are there elements that could be improved?

CHAPTER 6 THIRD PERIOD: THE APPLICATION

Create a Container

Choose one or two of the elements that you noted could be improved in the writing activity above, and brainstorm how you might implement those elements into your work and life. The first step may be in sharing these goals with others, or it may be taking on a new challenge, reflecting more regularly on our work and progress, or paving the way for a culture shift in how we think and speak about our work.

7

Honoring Our Alignment: A Montessori Approach to Time, Boundaries, and Negotiation

THE FEELING OF TIME PRESSURE, that I don't have enough time for all the things I want to do and be, has always been one of the greatest challenges to my alignment. It comes from a place of scarcity, of binary thinking, and of selfishness, being preoccupied with *my* time.

The Netflix series *Inventing Anna* has a particular scene that I found poignant. In it, the pregnant reporter Vivian Kent and her partner Jack are at the OB-GYN. The scene is already emotionally fraught, because Vivian had failed to attend the last appointment, caught up in her work, and Jack had been really looking forward to it. (He was less than thrilled with Vivian's priorities that day.) So in this rescheduled appointment, Jack and Vivian are about to find out the anatomical sex of their baby. Jack absolutely could not wait to learn more about the human they would welcome into their family. As the ultrasound technician moves the wand to bring up the images, a tiny person starts to come into view. The technician smiles and says, "Congratulations; it's a girl!"

Jack beams, elated.

Vivian, on the other hand, goes into what can only be described as an emotional fit.

She is completely overcome. She sobs and curses loudly. The technician is at a complete loss, with "what in the world" written all over her face. She excuses herself to "give them a minute." Jack is concerned about Vivian's emotional state and wants to understand what's happening for her, but he is also frustrated at the way her reaction is coloring what, for him, is a joyful moment.

In trying to explain herself, Vivian cries simply at first that now "She's real. She's real." When she's able to compose herself enough to say more, Vivian explains the tension she has been feeling between becoming a mother and her work as a reporter, which she feels isn't yet as established and credible as she wants it to be.

She says, "I thought I was going to have it fixed—my reputation. Before there is a tiny person I am required to keep alive and pay attention to. I want her; I do. It's just... I thought I would have my career saved. I thought it would be repaired, breathing, on its feet—before who I get to be changes."

She goes on to say, "I've run out of time, and if you tell me the joy of having a daughter is supposed to make up for the loss of my career, the loss of the thing that lights up my brain, I swear to God, I will smother you in your sleep."

To which Jack responds with a warm hug. They're okay, and the relationship is okay, but the tension between Jack's unambiguous excitement and Vivian's own ambivalence continues.

It's a poignant and relatable tension; a representation of multiple mosaic pieces, all of which matter deeply. Vivian is not sure what having a baby will mean for her work and her career, but she knows that her priorities will shift. She also says that she's "run out of time," implying that she doesn't see a way to continue in the satisfying work she loves (and redeem herself as a reporter) while also meeting the upcoming time demands of parenthood.

I won't dispute that when there's a "tiny person... to keep alive and pay attention to," time allocations change. This is true of most of our life changes: the demands on our time shift when there are changing health needs; changes in caretaking requirements for children, partners, parents, or pets; changes in our hobbies; or changes in our work.

Yet we have to find a way to move beyond the zero-sum approach of viewing our work as being in opposition to the nonwork parts of our lives. This is a huge part of what creates burnout: that feeling of scarcity. That no matter what, there's never enough: never enough time, never enough of *us*. But since we know change is inevitable, what if we could find a way throughout and in the midst of our life's changes to draw on the supportive alliance we've built among our work and nonwork pieces to strengthen our life's alignment, and to promote even greater overall thriving?

Because we cannot add even a single minute of extra time to our day, we have to consider how time impacts our alignment. Time is a key factor, maybe *the* key factor in our daily alignment.

The way we spend our time is the way we spend our lives, so aligning our lives cannot be separated from an examination of how we're spending our time. We feel out of alignment when we don't have the time we want to have for all our work and our nonwork pieces. And while time is a finite resource, the way we *perceive* time is malleable.

What would it mean to you to feel that you had all the time in the world for the things that matter? When was the last time that you went a full day without any time-bound obligations? Where the clock was for information only and not an indication of upcoming deadlines?

It can also be helpful to reflect on the lessons you've absorbed about time, which is a cultural construct. Some cultures utilize clock time, dividing the day into minutes and hours, with an emphasis on things happening at certain (reliable) times of the day. Japanese trains are legendary for their punctuality; any delay of over one minute is considered significant. But throughout human history, and even today, the experience of clock time is not universal. So what was your relationship with time growing up? Was time plentiful in your family? In your school? Did you spend most of your formative years rushing from one thing to another? Was punctuality important? Did events start at a specific time, or when everyone was present? Was there anything you particularly loved to do that always seemed to be cut short? Or were you allowed to take all the time that you needed to explore, create, understand, investigate?

A Montessori Perspective of Time

In a Montessori classroom, the "work cycle" is protected at all costs. While it looks a bit different for infants and toddlers as well as for adolescents, for children ages three to twelve, the work cycle is optimally a three-hour chunk of time where students have freedom to make choices about their learning and work, to work on something for a long time if they need to, and to have short lessons appropriate for the needs and development of each child. And while there are many benefits of the uninterrupted work cycle, including opportunities for deep concentration and flow, student empowerment, and an honoring of each student's unique pace and needs, this approach to work time for young people also supports the idea that there is enough. Students see that there is enough time. No bell will ring to force them to stop an activity and begin a new one. If I need to continue my work tomorrow, I will be able to. There are enough resources for everyone, even if we need to take turns. And where I am in my own development as a human is enough.

Not only that, Montessori classrooms help students understand deep time. We've already explored the idea of a cosmic approach; that each being in the universe has a cosmic task, a unique role to fulfill. That understanding is built for young children over the course of their Montessori education, with lessons and stories that show how the universe came to be, with a particular emphasis on helping students understand time. Timelines are present in every Montessori elementary classroom. One material, often called simply the "long black strip," offers an impressionistic lesson for students to understand how long the planet has existed and the relatively short time that humans have been a part of it. For the most accurate timeline, 46 meters (about 150 feet) of black felt is unrolled and unrolled for students, representing the 4.6 billion years that the Earth has existed. At the very end of the black fabric is a very small (half an inch or less) strip of red (or sometimes white) which represents the amount of time that humans have been on the planet. (Even at a quarter of an inch, the tiny strip is still generous, but it makes the point.) Students walk along the very long black strip, and they gain just a bit of perspective of how old the Earth is, and that it took a very, very long time for any humans to arrive on the planet!

From there, students might investigate other timelines, like the Timeline of Life, which also covers the history of the Earth, but with an introduction to major eras, and some examples of what life existed on the planet through the different periods. It emphasizes interdependence and how each species had an important role to play in the web of life, while also offering an understanding of human history as a relatively short period of time. There are also a variety of human timelines for students to explore how humans formed civilizations to meet basic needs; how civilizations have been connected throughout history offering an exchange of ideas, technology, and culture; and to show how human accomplishments like writing and mathematics were developed over time. These timelines give students a sense of connection and interconnection, and an understanding of common humanity and how humans are linked to the entire universe.

Even with such a large scale, Montessori students can also grow to understand clock time, as usually there is a start and end to the day, a time for lunch, etc. But what I have always loved about a Montessori perspective of time is that it shows time as vast, as spacious. All of humanity arrived when it was time, and not a moment sooner. My math project will take the time that it takes. I am enough, and I have enough time.

Changing Our Relationship with Time

Of course, I didn't have a Montessori educational experience growing up. In school, I learned that there was a finite amount of time to work on certain things, and when the deadline hit, my working time was over, regardless of how I felt about the product. Working quickly—something I became pretty good at doing—was generally valued in this system, though mistakes were not ideal, so speed might also be penalized if accuracy suffered. At home, though, at least in my younger years, I was gifted with a lot of uninterrupted time for free and imaginative play. Throughout my elementary and early middle school years, before the demands of "college prep" and organized sports really kicked in, I was free to explore the woods behind my house with neighborhood friends, ride bikes, climb trees, play street hockey, and more. (I also recognized that I was incredibly privileged to grow up in a location where these activities were generally safe, and with parents who didn't fear unsupervised play.) The family rule was that I should be home by the time the streetlights came on in the evenings. Summers were long, and I had the opportunity to work through boredom. I'm grateful that these opportunities gave me an alternative perspective to the scarcity mindset fostered at school, which was increasingly prevalent as I progressed through secondary school. My undergraduate studies offered somewhat more space again for thinking, growing, and becoming, at least in the seasons that I resisted complete overscheduling.

So how do we reconcile time pressures that we feel and the sense of abundance we want to have? What can we do to move towards a Montessori perspective of time?

One mantra that helped me to shift perspectives was to continually remind myself "I have all the time in the world." This reminds me of my connection to the infinite, and that I can trust that where I am at this moment is exactly where I am meant to be, doing what I am meant to be doing. Does that mean I don't plan or schedule? Definitely not. But it means that I have learned over the years to try to hold time, like other precious parts of my life, with open hands. Holding something precious with an open hand can feel risky, like you might drop it, or have it slip away. Like someone might take it. But when we hold something loosely, we can appreciate it more. We can look at it, share it with others, or receive more of it. If I clutch something tightly in a balled fist, I can't enjoy its beauty. I can't offer any to anyone else, and I can't receive any more of this particular blessing. I'm reduced to guarding my treasure, which may soon turn me, like the character Gollum in *The Lord of the Rings*, into a pitiable creature, disfigured by obsession for the precious item.

As I mentioned, holding time with open hands does, for me, still involve a decent amount of scheduling. I regularly preview and review my weeks and seasons. But when I'm engaged in reflection on my life's mosaic, and I'm clear on my highest priorities, my schedule is driven by these priorities more than the tyranny of a to-do list. When I can control my work schedule, I have learned to allow for some generous gaps in it, because more than ticking off every item on my list, I want to be able to answer the phone if a friend needs to talk for a bit. This means sometimes I have to be creative in when and how I work. However, I haven't always had a lot of control over when I do things during my working hours; most teachers and nurses I know don't. My paramedic friend spoke to this, too. There's no, "Oh, hey, I think I'll go take care of the heart attack guy at 2:00; that would fit much better with my schedule."

The other thing that changed my perspective of time was my noticing practice; specifically, noticing and focusing on where I actually was in the moment. It didn't give me more time, but it did change the way I related to it. This practice eventually helped me to be more present to bigger things, more focused on the person, place, or task at hand.

I hope this is well established by now, but it's still worth mentioning, that our brains literally cannot multitask. So not only is it impossible to do two significant cognitive tasks at once (like lesson planning or charting or writing a paper while also having a conversation about something else at the same time), it also usually leads to worse performance—increased errors and reduced productivity—as well as more fatigue. If I'm driving and going straight on a known, dry road with my cruise control on (lower cognitive load), I can carry on a conversation in the car without interruptions. But if the roads are unfamiliar, traffic is heavy, streets are wet or snowy, or there's some other complication, I won't talk and drive. I've learned this after seeing how many times I've missed a turn, even with GPS directions, because I've been engaged in a conversation with someone in the car.

If I'm having a conversation with someone, that's what I'm doing. Maybe also walking, or folding laundry, but not much else. Even if I'm watching TV, that's the thing that I'm doing. I don't have the TV on while I do other things; I don't scroll on my phone or carry on a text conversation while watching TV. (I'll pause it!) I'm either actively watching the show or movie, or I'm doing something else completely. And while I love music, music with lyrics engages my brain, because I love to listen and sing along. So music, for me, is usually for lower cognitive load activities, too, like making dinner, walking, driving, or housework.

Most of these habits came from my own noticings of how I felt at the end of the day or when I finished work. If I tried to multitask at work, the resulting errors just meant the tasks I was responsible for took twice as long. If I missed a turn while driving, it added time to my trip. Learning to notice and focus on where I am and what I'm doing in the moment has helped me protect the kind of deep work I want to be able to do.

But best of all, this learning to be present also helped me to be more attuned to the people and moments that matter most to me. If I'm spending time with a friend or family member, that's what I'm doing. I'm not also trying to write an email in my head. If I'm teaching, I'm teaching. I'm focused on the dynamics and engagement of the class, the learning, the energy. And if I'm on vacation, I'm on vacation, allowing my mind and body to fully reset, whether that's in exploring new places and cultures, catching up on my fun reading, or just marveling at a sunset. All of my mosaic pieces matter, and learning to be really present for them has led to greater connection to and joy from each precious piece.

Research bears this out. One amazing takeaway from a study of mindfulness for teachers was that teachers who had participated in mindfulness training that focused their attention on the present moment reported feeling significantly less time urgency than teachers who had not. Mindfulness didn't add any more hours to the day nor reduce the number of to-dos on teachers' lists. But it changed their relationship with time.

Oliver Burkeman's brilliant book, *Four Thousand Weeks: Time Management for Mortals* speaks to these ideas as well. The title comes from the average number of weeks a human lifetime contains; a person who lives to the age of seventy-seven will have 4,004 weeks on the planet. Of course, some of us have more time, and some of us have less. We never actually know which camp we'll fall into. Unlike most books on time management, Burkeman isn't offering advice on how we can fit more things into our day, accomplish more, be more here. Instead, he's urging us to do less. To embrace the limits of our time on the planet, and to focus our life energy on the things that really matter to us. I would say that Burkeman is urging us to evaluate our life's mosaic to find our most important pieces, and to prioritize them accordingly. He writes that we have to embrace the limits of what is possible and make peace with letting go of some things, and that the freedom to choose what really matters to us brings a new kind of peace and joy to our lives. This is living a life in alignment.

Boundaries and Negotiation

Our life mosaics are connected to others'. There are colleagues, family members, bosses, neighbors, friends, as well as clients, patients, and students in our lives. A shift we make in our own life mosaic will have an impact on them as well, and some will be more understanding and supportive of our realignment than others. So to be successful in honoring our alignment, we have to also look at how we communicate that alignment: our boundaries and negotiation.

A popular misconception about boundaries is that they're about other people. They're not. Boundaries are only ever for ourselves. As much as I sometimes wish it were otherwise, *we* are the only ones we can control. But we can negotiate with others!

There are two principles of Montessori classrooms that I think can help us with our boundaries and negotiation. The first idea, "freedom within limits" (which is sometimes expressed a variety of different ways), can help us set boundaries. The second idea, "navigating rights and responsibilities," can help us with negotiation. We'll explore the latter concept a little further on, but first, let's look at boundaries.

One of the biggest misconceptions that folks sometimes have about Montessori education is that students are allowed to do whatever they want. Parents worry that if that's the case, how will any learning happen? What if my child never wants to do any math? Without getting into all the ways a trained and expert teacher can guide students to make sure that no area of their holistic development is neglected, I'll just explain this guiding principle: students are offered specific freedoms within appropriate limits. This means that while choices are prevalent, not everything is a choice. Students may choose the material (the "work") they would like to engage with, but not all materials are always available. First, students may not use a material until they have had a lesson on it. Second, students are not permitted to take a material that another student is currently using. Third, they have to finish with a material and put it away before they may choose another material.

I like to think of boundaries in our lives as representing freedom within limits. I, along with every other human in my life, am free to make choices and act, just like students in a Montessori classroom. There are also laws, customs, and personal values that guide (and limit) my actions and choices. And there are limits to the choices and actions I will accept from others, and I can make these limits clear by my own responses to their choices and actions. For example, I had a supervisor once who made me uncomfortable. I couldn't exactly put my finger on the issue, but somehow, I just didn't feel safe with him. He was physically large, and sometimes it seemed like he used his size in an attempt to literally "throw his weight around." I got the impression that he was not used to people (smaller, women) disagreeing with him or challenging his thinking. I've also been fortunate to live a life where I haven't had too many occasions where someone tried to physically hurt me, so it's not an alarm that goes off in my head very often. I've had just enough occasions, though, that I've learned to be aware of my situation and to trust my gut when things don't feel right. (*The Gift of Fear* by Gavin de Becker emphasizes a similar approach.)

So, although our relationship started off okay, I quickly got the sense that this supervisor didn't really like me. Maybe there was an element of intimidation, maybe there was annoyance that I spoke my mind, or maybe it was all in my head. There was one time when he asked to speak with me privately that I realized things didn't feel right. The interaction didn't last long, and it never even got heated. But it was the last time I ever spoke to him alone, because that was the day I set a boundary for our working relationship. Even if he had something negative to say about me or my work, I decided that day that I would rather take the risk of feeling embarrassed by having another person hear him than feel unsafe. I would rather have a witness, so if there was a difference in accounts, it wouldn't be a he-said-she-said situation, where I had less clout. So I set the boundary of making sure I was never alone with him. He was free to speak with me, and the limit to that freedom (that I got to decide!) was to insist on someone else being present as well. I was not in control of his choices or actions, what he might do or say, but I was in charge of my own. And my boundary provided me with a safe limit to the situation.

The key is, the boundary is about choosing what you will do in advance, because we can't control other people. So, if you have a family member who is challenging for you, the limit to their freedom might be that you see or speak with them once per month, and no more. If there's a topic you don't wish to discuss, you say that you're not going to discuss that again, then change the subject or leave the room, as many times as that takes. Others are always going to be free to do what they're going to do. But boundaries are for ourselves, limiting the impact of other people's choices and actions on our lives.

Negotiations follow a similar principle. If boundaries are about "freedom within limits," negotiations are, as I mentioned, about the Montessori principle of "navigating rights and responsibilities." The two ideas are similar, but not the same.

The Montessori principle of rights and responsibilities speaks to the lessons students learn in the classroom community that everyone matters, and everyone is expected to behave in a way that furthers their own learning and contributes positively to those around them. For example, students have the right to choose the materials they want to work with, and they have the responsibility of putting materials back where they belong and generally restoring the environment back to its original state of cleanliness. Students have the right to feel seen and heard, safe and valued in their classroom, and they have the responsibility to make sure that others feel the same.

While the idea of freedom within limits highlights personal autonomy (independence), the principle of rights and responsibilities emphasizes the interdependence of the classroom community. That's where negotiation comes in.

I've been married for over twenty years to a human I love very much. And, like all human pairings, we've had to communicate our needs and differences. When we're both in a healthy place, this usually happens pretty seamlessly. Even if just one of us is in a good place, we are able to navigate the give-and-take pretty well; I've already mentioned that it's normal for us to completely change up household contributions, based on the stress level and workload of other areas of our lives.

However, there is one place we can always do better, and that's when we're both in the position of being stressed by things that fall more within our individual, rather than shared, mosaic pieces... like our paycheck work. (If we're facing something hard that's shared, we tend to do better.) My stress response when I have too much going on is often to look around and say, "Why isn't anyone helping me? If anyone really cared about me, they would ask how they could help. Actually, they would just open their eyes and do the thing that very obviously needs doing, rather than waiting for me to tell them." I forget in these moments that the "very obvious" things might only be obvious to me. (Except dishes. Surely everyone can see dishes!) My beloved's stress response when he has too much going on is to say, "I need everyone to stop bothering me. I swear, if one more person makes one more demand of me, I'm going to lose it."

So you can see how both of us having a stressful time at the same time can quickly become a problem. I would feel frustrated that he wasn't being responsive to my needs and that he was retreating when I felt that I needed his support the most. He would feel frustrated that he had more and more demands from me at exactly the time that he was feeling the most depleted. Not only that, but these additional demands were coming from the person who was supposed to have *his* back.

We both know that when life's timing works out this way, it's a hard place for us. But even though *we know* the pattern, it can still lead to frustration for each of us. We both have the right to have our needs met. And we both have the responsibility to support each other. These rights and responsibilities... this is the heart of negotiating our alignment.

When these stress responses first appeared in our marriage, one thing that helped (as it usually does) was an honest discussion when we weren't in our stressed states. We could talk about where the feelings come from, why we believe what we believe when we're stressed, and what we most want from each other.

I was able to communicate that I don't want to feel like a burden to my partner, especially since I can struggle to ask for help and support anyway. But the beautiful part of having a life partner means that I'm not all alone. I'm allowed to ask for things from him that I would not ask of a mere friend. We're committed to each other in a different way, so I'm allowed to be vulnerable, to ask for help, and to expect responsiveness from my partner.

In return, I had to recognize that my asks, especially if they felt like demands, were hard for him when he was already feeling maxed out. He needed to have his autonomy supported and his contributions recognized. If they weren't, his default was to withdraw.

I won't say that this dynamic never presents itself anymore, because it is probably something we'll always have to be attuned to. But when we can both recognize our own rights and responsibilities, we can negotiate a workable solution, own our own missteps or default reactions, and work towards the healthier dynamic that we both want.

There's no way around it: communicating and honoring our alignment is going to require boundaries and negotiation. When setting a boundary, remember that it's simply the limit you're putting into place. You can't control others, so the limit is your own response when someone's freedoms extend a little too far.

Negotiations are about communicating openly and honestly about each person's rights and responsibilities. You have a responsibility to your students, patients, clients, colleagues, supervisors. And you have the right to attend to other important pieces of your life mosaic as well. You have a right to disconnect from paycheck work, a right to say no to additional responsibilities, and a right to show up and be seen in your full humanity. Sometimes negotiations fail, if one or both parties can't agree on the reasonable rights and responsibilities. When that's the case, those aren't healthy relationships to be in, and we can use our boundaries to set limits to (or, sometimes, remove ourselves from) those connections.

CHAPTER 7 SECOND PERIOD: THE PRACTICE

Writing Activity

I always seem to want more time for the things that matter, but it can be helpful to remember that life has certain seasons. You may be in a season where caregiving requires a significant portion of your time, or you may find that your paycheck work is more demanding in certain months. For this writing activity, I want you to consider your priorities in this season of your life.

1. Start by listing 10 to 20 important pieces of your current life mosaic. (You can look at your list from Chapter 1, but it might be interesting to work from the top of your head now and see if/how your list has changed.)

2. Consider your schedule over the last day, week, and month (if you keep a calendar or planner, you might refer to that to jog your memory, too). Then, looking at each piece on your list, note whether you feel that the time you've given each piece is insufficient, adequate, or excessive, considering your current needs and responsibilities.

3. Finally, if you'd like your time to better reflect your current life mosaic, brainstorm what you'd like the next week (or month) to look like.

Reflection Questions

- How did you experience time growing up? Was it a scarce resource? Did you often feel hurried? Or did you have opportunities to experience time as vast and plentiful? Did events start at a certain time, or did events start when everyone was present?

- If time pressure is a source of stress in your life, how can you change your relationship with time, maybe to a more "open-handed" approach?

- There's good research to show that slowing down and staying present to one thing at a time, paradoxically, can help us feel that we have more time. What are some areas of your life or work where you might implement "solotasking" (as opposed to multitasking)?

- Communicating and honoring our alignment will require both boundaries and negotiation. Where have you been successful with these elements in the past? Is there a part of your life or work now that would benefit from a boundary or some (re)negotiation?

- Remember that boundaries are always about our own reactions to the behavior of others, because we cannot control the actions and choices of other people. If there is a challenging person or situation in your life that you think would be helped by implementing a boundary (providing a limit), can you brainstorm *what your own approaches* to the problematic behavior or situation could be?

CHAPTER 7 THIRD PERIOD: THE APPLICATION

Honoring Your Alignment
Choose one or more of the following:

- Implement a boundary by choosing what your own responses will be to a person or situation that is negatively impacting your life.

- Open a negotiation with someone by asking for a conversation to discuss how you might mutually consider one another's rights and responsibilities.

- Practice solotasking as often as possible for a week and notice whether or how it changes your relationship with time.

- Review your writing activity above and implement your time/schedule brainstorm for the coming week or month.

8

Our Ever-Changing Mosaics: Navigating Change and Grief

LEARNING TO ALIGN AND REALIGN our life mosaic is empowering. It reminds us that wherever we are, we have the power to focus on the things that matter most to us. That we aren't stuck in a situation, whether it's a job, a relationship, or a bad habit. Aligning and realigning is all about making positive changes, so that we can find joy and thriving in our lives, for the rest of our lives.

Of course, not all change is equal, not all change is under our control, and not all change is positive. So, while I believe that no matter what life brings, you still have the power to choose your responses and to arrange your life mosaic pieces as *you* see fit; we can't feel confident in our alignment unless we also feel confident in managing and supporting the inevitable changes that happen throughout our lives.

The alignment process, of course, already includes change. In step three, we ask ourselves whether we need an internal shift, changes that we make within, or an external shift, changes that we need in our environment. But making internal changes isn't always easy, and advocating for external changes doesn't always bring the results we want.

And there's another kind of change to address as well, and those are changes that we didn't choose but that our life mosaic has to absorb. It might be the result of someone else's choice, or it might just be something that happens: a diagnosis, an accident. Depending on scope, these unchosen changes can have a huge impact on our alignment. Some changes may seem to break, or even shatter, our life mosaics. These kinds of changes are the cause of grief in our lives, a human reaction to loss.

So this chapter, dear reader, is all about supporting and navigating changes in and to our life mosaic, in order to support a healthy alignment. This topic could be a book unto itself (or even three) in addressing these three types of changes. And anyone feeling really stuck may need a deeper dive than what this chapter can provide. But since none of the books I've ever read on change and grief specifically address our holistic life alignment, I hope this chapter will bridge the ideas. Feel free to read the whole chapter in order, or to skip straight to the sections that feel most relevant, helpful, or important to you right now.

The first section will address internal changes that we *want to make*, things we either want to start or stop doing. The second section will address external changes we *want to advocate for*, and the final section will address navigating the inevitable life changes that we *didn't want at all*, including the painful experience of human grief.

Internal Shifts

Internal shifts are changes that you have control over; you don't need anyone else to make them or their permission to do them. As I mentioned in Chapter 5, these kinds of shifts can be changes to attitude, thought patterns, or self-talk. They can include learning a new skill, implementing a new habit, or starting to organize aspects of our lives differently. That doesn't make them easy, because if they were easy, we would all keep our New Year's resolutions perfectly, we would all only ever engage in positive self-talk, and we would never procrastinate about our work.

However, internal changes are the most powerful ways to align and realign our lives, because we *do* have control over them. Remember how boundaries, the limits we apply to the freedom of others, are actually about our own behaviors and responses? Whether we like it or not, we are the only ones we can control in life.

There have been many great books written about how we humans can start or stop doing things. *Atomic Habits* by James Clear, *Better Than Before* by Gretchen Rubin, *The Power of Habit* by Charles Duhigg, and *Tiny Habits* by BJ Fogg all offer some really useful (and generally science-backed) advice about how to start building healthy habits or how to replace unhealthy habits.

I won't try to synthesize all these authors' advice here, but what I did notice in many of these books is that there are a ton of connections (again) to a Montessori classroom. Change experts tell us that to make changes easy, we should make them fun, make them meaningful, make them obvious, and more. Those are all great practices! But I see making positive changes in our lives as another way of supporting our own human development. So just as I discussed in Chapter 6, supporting internal change requires a developmental container, and a Montessori classroom can model the principles to help us create one. Our developmental container for making changes needs to offer us three things: intrinsic motivation, a prepared environment, and community.

First, changes that are the most long-lasting tap into our intrinsic motivation. They are connected to our why. Whatever it is that we're trying to start doing or stop doing, it has to be tied to our life's alignment, the mosaic pieces that matter to us (this can help make the change satisfying). We're not going to really get anywhere with "should." You may think, for example, that you *should* want to lose weight, get stronger, or increase your cardiovascular fitness. But unless your body (and thus its care) is actually an important piece of your life mosaic, all the *shoulds* in the world aren't really going to motivate you. So, if you're trying to connect the change you want to a deeper why but don't already feel a lot of intrinsic motivation, see if you can connect the change to a mosaic piece you care about.

For at least the last decade, I've known that lifting weights (specifically) would be a good thing for me to do. I knew that as a woman with small bones and a family history of osteoporosis and osteopenia that lifting weights could make a difference in my bone health. But it was reading the book *Outlive* by Peter Attia that convinced me that if I want to be able to hike, ski, and travel into my old age, building muscle and bone mass *now* is the only way to align my present self with the active future I want. It's those mosaic pieces, the active hobbies and traveling, because they connect me to my loved ones, to nature, and to new adventures, that I most want to protect.

Montessori classrooms know the importance of intrinsic motivation, and they go to great lengths to nurture and protect it in students. These classrooms were supporting student autonomy, competence, and relatedness before Richard Ryan and Edward Deci's self-determination theory, which I explored in Chapter 4, was even articulated. They do this in offering choices (autonomy), opportunities to be successful and learn from mistakes (competence), and helping students see how their contributions matter to others (relatedness). We can build on these ideas to form healthy habits when we fully own the choices we make around our internal changes, when we celebrate our wins and view our setbacks as learning opportunities, and when we connect our changes to others, which I will discuss further in the external changes section.

Second, our developmental container needs a prepared (supportive) environment for the successful implementation of changes (this can help make the change easier). To make a new change stick, we will find much more success if we make it easy. A Montessori classroom places a huge emphasis on having a prepared environment, because students will learn from the environment itself. That means materials are attractive, so that students want to work with them. It means that the environment is organized, so students can easily see where to go and get what they need. And it means that the environment is set up to prevent behaviors that are less desired; students know where in the classroom they can go (and often have tools available to help them) if they are feeling emotionally dysregulated and need to calm down or resolve a conflict.

When we prepare our own environments, we're trying to make our changes easier, more automatic, or more attractive/enjoyable. When I got serious about writing, I set up three different locations where I could write in the mornings. Each one of them has an external keyboard and mouse trackpad, a mug-warmer to keep my tea or coffee at the correct temperature, and two additional coasters for water or other beverages. They all also have a good-smelling candle, little knick-knacks (pictures of or notes from loved ones, travel souvenirs, and other things that make me happy), plus sticky notes, pens, lip balm, hand lotion, and tissues. In addition to making my writing locations more pleasant, which makes me more excited to spend time there, the environment has everything I need, so that I'm not off searching for a pen or tissue, which would take me away from the task at hand. Then, if I program the coffee maker the night before and fill my water glass, I am even more committed to my morning. Similarly, if you're trying to make changes to your habits to embrace a healthier lifestyle, the common advice of packing your gym bag and laying out your gym clothes the night before is another way to prepare your environment to make the healthy choice easier. And limiting the junk food you bring into the house is a way of preparing your environment to be less supportive of a behavior you don't want. Willpower is a finite resource. If we prepare the environment to better support the behaviors we do want, and to be less supportive of the behaviors we don't want, to reduce the possible choices we have to make or friction between us and our goal, our changes and healthy habits are more likely to stick.

Finally, changes are best implemented in community, where we have the opportunity to learn from others a little further along, where we can find encouragement, and where we're held accountable (this can help make the change fun). We can engage community to support our changes. A hallmark of a Montessori classroom is a mixed-age environment; students typically spanning three years in age are together in one classroom. This is a way to support each student's individual development, rather than assuming that all students of a given age are in the same place developmentally. It also means that students learn from each other. Younger students observe and can imitate the older ones, older ones can model and give lessons to the younger ones. And as students get older, the give-and-take in a Montessori classroom becomes less about chronological age, and more about experience, skill mastery, and skill readiness. All students experience the opportunity to both give and receive support from their classmates, regardless of how old they are. The classroom community wishes for, and celebrates, the successes of everyone. And everyone is held accountable for their contributions.

When we are trying to implement changes in our lives, we don't need to go it alone. An exercise class, team, or partner can make a huge difference in helping us implement healthy habits. Reporting our goals and progress to a friend, asking for support and accountability, can also help keep us on track. And asking for a lesson or advice when we're feeling stuck, gaining wisdom from someone who has been where we are, can keep us from stalling out completely.

But not everything is an internal change. And if we're going to protect and promote our life's healthy alignment (and, I would argue, the alignment of others) we sometimes need external shifts as well.

External Shifts

External changes, unlike internal ones, are changes that we can't make happen all on our own. These are changes in our environment, and they require support from or collaboration with other humans. This doesn't mean that we're powerless to effect these kinds of changes; we always have choices, including setting our own boundaries. In fact, there are a number of folks who would rather work on external changes than internal ones! And just like the concept of negotiation that I discussed in Chapter 7, external changes are best considered within the Montessori framework of rights and responsibilities.

Rights and responsibilities are also at the heart of what Harvard philosopher T.M. Scanlon describes as "contractualism," an approach to interpersonal morality that is captured by his book's title, *What We Owe to Each Other*. The TV show *The Good Place* features this concept prominently as well; show creator Michael Schur remarked in an interview that "you owe certain things to the people that you share Earth with and that's the point of the show, very explicitly." In the show, characters find that friendship and working together, true interdependence, are the only ways to save humanity and themselves.

In a Montessori classroom, students learn that everyone has rights and everyone has responsibilities to the whole. Students learn to advocate for themselves and others. At younger levels, Montessori students are encouraged to name their feelings, to take breaks when they need to, and to engage in peaceful conflict resolution. At the older ages, students continue to learn conflict resolution, teaming strategies, and they have regular community meetings to discuss needs, share decision-making, and celebrate one another. Montessori students are also encouraged to be changemakers beyond the classroom, in their middle and high schools, in their local communities, and in the wider world as they explore how they might use their talents to be of service in the world.

To effect changes outside of themselves, Montessori students practice collaborative problem-solving, establishing and upholding group norms, articulating a compelling argument, as well as how to be of service, how to advocate on behalf of themselves and others, and how to build consensus.

There's no easy answer to effect change, especially external changes. But we can draw on the principles of interdependence, of rights and responsibilities. So, whether your external change requires negotiating with just one other person, like a partner or colleague, or a group of people, like a team, a whole organization, or even a whole system, the first steps are the same.

First, we have to be clear on what we want and need. That includes being clear on our own boundaries, too, with a plan for what *we* will do if we're not able to effect the change we want. If we want change, it's much more powerful to propose a vision for what we *do* want as opposed to simply fighting against what we *don't* want. Activist and author Dr. Shawn A. Ginwright describes this when he says, "eliminating things that harm us is not the same as creating things that heal us. Just like the absence of disease does not constitute health... ending these problems does little to cultivate the world we really want." So if there's a change you want or need, spend time with what you really do want, not just what don't want.

Second, we have to give voice to our wants and needs. Here, even if your goal is to effect change in a larger group, organization, or society, it helps to start small. Share with one person, two people, three people. Build a coalition, a network. And if your desired change only involves a handful of people, remember that they can't read your mind. We have to have some boldness.

Third, bring people along. Most of the humans you interact with are not likely to be complete monsters. If there's a blind spot, help them to see it. Speak your truth. Share your story. Do your best to assume good intent. And remember that all relationships, all community, has to be grounded in give-and-take, in our interdependence. Show your understanding of rights and responsibilities, your commitment to the well-being of the whole.

After my sister Abby's realization that work wasn't the only issue in her life, she set about making some changes. First, however, she spent some significant time with herself to tune into her deepest wants and needs for this stage of her life. There's no shortcut for this part; Abby had some grief and identity work to process. She did a lot of journaling, walking, and thinking. It was more than just a little hard time, and it wasn't something that was accomplished in a day, a week, or even a month. But as Abby did this deep reflecting, she started to uncover the next right things for herself, to realign both her work and her nonwork mosaic pieces.

She made a lot of internal shifts to her nonwork pieces, including a commitment to intentionally spend time on things that brought her joy. She continued her commitment to exercise and healthy eating, setting up Zoom workouts with friends and loved ones and trying out new recipes. When she had a day off, she arranged to meet friends or family members outdoors, where she wouldn't be worried about a COVID exposure and inadvertently risking the safety of her patients. And she bought a bigger bed to help her get the best sleep possible. (We laugh that while I typically sleep with one pillow, Abby prefers five.)

And she made some internal and external shifts to her work pieces, too. With her deep noticing, Abby realized that what she loved most about being an oncology nurse was when she was able to provide holistic support to both patients and their families. Nurses are trained to look at the whole patient, but this was also the part of her job that was often limited by time in her hospital work. There simply wasn't always enough time to process a patient's emotional needs, to talk through nutritional choices, or to prepare them for what may lie ahead when she always had a full patient assignment. There were always at least three or four other human beings, each with extensive needs and potential crises, who needed her attention. Abby realized that she also only ever got to work with patients in a particular phase of their cancer treatment; when they left the hospital, the relationship was over. And yet, she wasn't ready to walk away from this work.

Eventually, Abby realized that what she most wanted was the opportunity to see and learn some new things, and to build a career that allowed her to forge deeper relationships with patients. So Abby invested in some new learning opportunities for herself and started a nurse health coaching program, with classes and a practicum that she completed outside of her full-time work over the course of a year. And without a furry friend at home anymore, she left her current hospital and took the opportunity to work as a traveling nurse for two years, but only to locations where she already had close friends and family. Both experiences added to her professional expertise, and while she enjoyed some travel assignments more than others, this time of deep learning and reconnecting to herself only strengthened her healthy alignment.

Today, Abby is thriving in her work and life, joyfully living her cosmic task of providing compassionate care to those touched by cancer. She has returned to her work as a floor nurse at the same hospital, but with reduced hours, so that her work is enhanced by the deeper relationships she now forges with patients and caregivers as an oncology nurse coach. And of course, her life mosaic will continue to evolve!

Unchosen Changes and Grief

Here's the hard truth: All the individual pieces that make up our beautiful life mosaic are temporary. We might be lucky enough to hold on to some of our precious pieces for the rest of our lives, but that's not guaranteed. No one expects or wants to outlive their children, but it sometimes happens. Spouses, pets, and best friends die. Jobs and hobbies evolve with changing time and technology and with our own abilities. Our bodies change as we age. As I mentioned at the beginning of this chapter, these kinds of changes may seem to break, or even shatter, our life mosaics. They are the cause of grief in our lives, a human reaction to loss.

I have learned to consider myself "temporarily able bodied," a fact that, when I can call it to consciousness, reminds me of my connection to all those in the disability world. A favorite poem that reminds me of this is called "Otherwise" by Jane Kenyon, where she recalls simple beautiful facts about her day—waking up, doing work she loves, spending time with her partner, recognizing all the while how fortunate it is to be doing these simple acts of living, working, and loving, because it could have been, and indeed someday will be, "otherwise."

The Latin phrase "carpe diem" is well known in our culture, an exhortation to seize the day. But the Romans were equally fond of another phrase "memento mori," which is best translated as "remember to die." In fact, these phrases went together. Remembering that you will die was not a morbid idea, but simply, like Kenyon's understanding of "otherwise," an acknowledgment that we do have today, today is a gift because we might not have tomorrow, and so we should take advantage of it. Carpe diem is the logical outflow of memento mori.

As much as I wish this weren't true, we simply don't have control over all the pieces in our life mosaic. Some pieces are added, and we have to deal with them. They weren't carefully chosen, not part of our original plan for our lives. They could be small, like an annoying work assignment that's taking up too much time. Or they could be pieces that are so large, they require a radical realignment of our life mosaic, like a life-changing diagnosis for ourselves or someone we love and care for.

I recall an amazing podcast with Brené Brown where she discussed grief as being particularly scary to her. I recall feeling comforted, because the inevitable losses still to come in my life can be frightening to me as well. But I also think that we can make the mistake of only thinking about grief in the most catastrophic terms, situations where we might endure (and grieve) the worst losses we can imagine. I remember when my husband expressed more than a little concern that I, along with all the other members of my immediate family plus partners were booked together on a single flight without him. Imagining something happening to all of us at once was not a happy consideration for him.

But the fact is, in the same way that therapists and others often recognize that we can have "Big T" Trauma and "little t" trauma, we can also have big grief and more minor grief, which sometimes goes unrecognized. Grief is our human reaction to loss. The loss can be concrete (loss of a person, pet, home, job) or it can be more abstract: loss of a relationship, loss of a part of our identity, or loss of an imagined future that will no longer be possible.

And change, which we know is constant in our lives, also involves losses. Even positive changes, joyful changes, bring with them the shadows of some losses. The joyful birth of a longed-for child still brings changes to identity and lifestyle for parents, including a loss of previously "free" time. A joyful and triumphant graduation means the loss of familiar routines and people, relationships that are sure to change. A long-awaited and well-earned retirement can bring a loss of routine, relationships, and sometimes identity. And I think we often forget to reflect on that side of the coin.

We probably all know some people who seem especially averse to change. I know, in the context of my employment, I've been frustrated by such approaches (and I'm sure I've frustrated others when I have been change-resistant myself!). But perhaps there's a place for a helpful reframe. Perhaps our friends who most "don't like change" are the friends who feel the grief that change brings even more poignantly. Maybe they're more attuned to it that way, to see both the beauty of possibility for the new thing but also the brutality of loss for the old thing. Maybe we can learn to be patient with those friends, and with ourselves when we're in that space as well. Change is constant in our lives, but even when we choose the change, it isn't always easy.

The other problem with only thinking about the most catastrophic losses is it sets up a comparison, a kind of grief Olympics, where losses are compared and rated. But first of all, we can never truly know another person's experience. And second, grief and loss are part of the human experience. Comparing separates us. It makes us think that "my" grief is bigger than "your" grief (or vice versa) and so we "shouldn't complain." But all our feelings are meant to be felt, as many wise teachers before me have stated. And I believe that if we let it, recognizing and sharing this human experience of grief, the loss that comes for each one of us can help us to feel more connected to each other and to ourselves. Each person does navigate their own grief in their own way. But the feeling of loss itself? That is universal. It is what comes of having a great love. And human societies have long held elaborate rituals to mark and move through grief. Where the community comes together to publicly acknowledge the loss, feel the feelings, and support those most impacted.

Some of these markers, though, have been de-emphasized in our culture, so when we are faced with grief, it can be difficult to know where to turn. And some would prefer to skip the markers of grief altogether, as though that would make the feelings less present. But skipping a funeral doesn't make the grief go away.

I'm honored to call Edy Nathan, an expert on grief and trauma, a friend. In her first book, *It's Grief*, Edy shares practical ways for someone to move through any kind of grief, including the need to engage with it, to give yourself permission to heal at your own pace, to draw on support systems, and to create a personal toolkit of practices that can help ground, reconnect, and support healing.

And because grief and trauma are often connected in complicated ways, the book *Trauma Stewardship: An Everyday Guide to Caring for Self While Caring for Others*, by Laura van Dernoot Lipsky, offers important wisdom for how folks can stay connected to meaningful work that can also be a source of pain. It's written for professionals in fields like social work and healthcare, such as first responders, activists, teachers, and others who make the world a better place. It seems we're learning more and more about secondary trauma in the helping professions, and van Dernoot Lipsky does an incredible job addressing the impact that helping professions can have on individuals, with a goal of helping us identify trauma responses that may present themselves. Because if we can notice them, "trauma stewardship" can also help us find new ways to frame and escape our trauma responses, so that we can continue to care for ourselves, others, and the causes that matter most to us.

As with other changes we might want to implement, it is impossible to prescribe an exact set of tools to work through changes we didn't choose, especially if they are complicated by grief. But what we can do is give ourselves time and space, practice our noticing, and start to discern how our mosaic pieces will come back together. When our life mosaic feels broken, whether it's a minor chip or a major shattering, it's going to take time to learn how our pieces will fit back together again. But they will. The remaining pieces may not fit the same way as before; there may be new pieces to make room for, maybe with more aligning work to do, but our precious and unique life mosaics can still be beautiful.

CHAPTER 8 SECOND PERIOD: THE PRACTICE

Writing Activity

Journal about any internal shifts you're still considering (you might review previous journal responses) that would likely enhance your life's healthy alignment.

Then journal about any external shifts you would like to advocate for, that would promote your own thriving (and very likely the thriving of others as well).

For both journals, try to focus on what you do want, rather than what you don't want.

Reflection Questions

- How can you connect the internal shifts you want to make to your own sense of meaning and purpose, to your why, to your cosmic task? Can you build in elements of autonomy, competence, or relatedness? Can you make the shift easier, more automatic, or more enjoyable? Can you tap into a community of some kind for support with this change?

- Sometimes people find it difficult to journal about desired shifts in terms of what they want, as opposed to focusing on what they don't want. If this was true for you, you might spend some time thinking about the best possible outcome or situation you can imagine for that shift and work backwards from there. What would it take to get there? What small steps can you take now?

- What are your most baseline reactions to change in your life? If you have ever noticed a grief response to change, how can you engage with that feeling and give yourself permission to heal at your own pace?

CHAPTER 8 THIRD PERIOD: THE APPLICATION

Navigating Change
Choose one or more of the following:

- Work on implementing one of the internal shifts you journaled about, using the first reflection question to help you.

- Make a plan to advocate for an external shift you'd like to see and find a partner to help you implement your plan.

- If you're in the midst of grieving a loss, give yourself time and space. As you keep practicing your noticing, you'll start to discern how your mosaic pieces will come back together. It might be different from before, but it can still be beautiful.

9

Your Alignment Matters: Our Interconnected Mosaics

NO ONE IS MORE SURPRISED than me that I wrote this book. Not because figuring out my life's alignment, learning to align and realign my life, has been a journey. That's how alignment goes, because our lives have seasons, and change is constant.

No, it's because the first seedling idea for this book wasn't about an individual's life alignment. It was an idea for communities of people, like workplaces. It was about systems.

And perhaps that book will still come to fruition someday. Systems are powerful because they create environments, ecosystems. And I believe that each one of us is a part of many systems and environments that create our overall life ecosystem. I also believe we can create these environments, or containers, for ourselves, as discussed in Chapter 6.

But not only that, I believe that our interconnected ecosystems need to be in alignment as well, where the big pieces that make up those elements are in, as the first definition of alignment states, the "correct or appropriate relative positions." Our workplaces, our families, our friendship networks can all find alignment. Because, although this book is written for individuals, the fact of the matter is that none of us do big things alone. When we thrive, it is because we are in situations that support thriving. Our mosaics don't stand alone; they are inextricably linked to other people and their mosaics as well.

As one tiny illustration of the point, I loved learning that one happy person not only impacts the happiness of people closest to them, they also impact the happiness of people to three degrees of separation. That means, if I am a happy person, I'm likely to increase the happiness of people closest to me. And their increased happiness is likely to increase the happiness of those closest to them. But even the friends of my friends' friends are likely to have an increase in their happiness levels if I am a happy person. We are impacted by the affective states of people we likely don't even know! All because they are connected to a friend of a friend of a friend.

In Montessori teacher education, as I've shared, we often talk about independence and interdependence. Independence is a well-known aim, because it is such a critical part of the education of very young people, who still comprise the majority of Montessori schools and programs. Indeed, Maria Montessori wrote that "help me to do it alone" is the cry of the young child. But as humans grow up, the aim starts to shift to helping them see where they fit into the broader human society. I like to say that the point of all the early emphasis on independence is so that students can then learn how to be interdependent. If I don't learn the early skills of independence, of taking responsibility for my actions, I'm not going to be a dependable link in our interdependent network. If I don't spend time honing my own skills, talents, and passions,

I won't know how to contribute them to the greater good. An early emphasis on independence can set the stage for understanding and appreciating our true nature of interdependence.

In *Braiding Sweetgrass*, Robin Wall Kimmerer wrote about this approach as well in her chapter "Allegiance to Gratitude." She wrote that students at the Onondaga Nation School begin their weeks with the Thanksgiving Address, which grounds students in all that there is to be thankful for and a culture of reciprocity. She wrote that an Onondaga teacher explained to her that the address also teaches young people "that much is expected of them eventually... Like the maple, leaders are the first to offer their gifts." Kimmerer goes on to explain that "cultures of gratitude must also be cultures of reciprocity. Each person... is bound to every other in a reciprocal relationship. Just as all beings have a duty to me, I have a duty to them."

When it comes to aligning our lives around our purpose work, our cosmic task, what we are here to do and be right now, we gain a cosmic vision. This is, as author and social change advocate Ulcca Joshi Hansen explained in her presentation at the Montessori Event 2023, closer to a holistic-Indigenous perspective—like the one Kimmerer outlines—than it is to the traditional Cartesian-Newtonian worldview, where all things can be reduced to their parts. Because it is a holistic approach.

We are whole humans, living our whole lives. And just like a Montessori environment strives to nurture the whole student, meeting their intellectual, emotional, physical, social, and spiritual needs, so we, too, need to attend to all our precious mosaic pieces. Our alignment matters, because *we* matter. We each have a gift to give, a cosmic task, a place in the universe.

With a cosmic approach, there is a sense of wonder and awe. Time is vast. Children learn that everything in the universe is working as a part of something even bigger. Adjectives are working to describe a noun, wind is working to distribute heat on the planet. Children see that the point of work is to learn, to grow, and to contribute to a greater whole, and that we each have a role to play. And it leads to a series of natural explorations, around questions of *What is my work?* and *How can I contribute?*

Children see the interconnectedness of all things, and they also learn about how resources can be shared in ways that promote the well-being of the whole. Equity practitioner and coach Maati Wafford taught me (and other Montessori professionals) an example of this from anatomy. She reminded us how even in our own bodies, we see justice and equitable approaches as part of a deep interdependence. If I step on something sharp and cut my foot, there will be a whole series of internal changes that happen. My body will send a host of resources to the site of the wound, to give it what it needs and try to begin the healing process. This is justice: when needs are met. And it happens because the foot is not separate from the rest of the body. Even though a human can live without a foot, the brain doesn't say "good thing that wasn't me" and move on. Nor does it say, well, it's not fair to send more resources and energy to the foot than to the hands, because hands matter, too. No, the body recognizes wholeness. The foot is a part of the body, and so it must get the resources that it needs when it needs them. (This is equity.)

There's a funny thing that can happen when our work is part of how we make a difference in the world. We forget that our interconnectedness literally means that resources and energy must flow both out and in. This is what can save us from ourselves, from our martyr or savior complexes.

And I know you know what I'm talking about. The martyr complex, where we feel we must sacrifice everything for the cause. We deny ourselves sleep, food, downtime. Or the savior complex, where everything is up to me, because if I don't take care of everything, clearly no one else can or will. These two approaches are both rooted in disconnection and ego. In these states, we compare schedules to see who is busier, we take pride in our self-sacrifice, our selflessness.

Many of us are comfortable giving of ourselves to areas of greatest need in our work and our lives. But we forget to measure ourselves and our own needs when taking stock. And if we are truly interconnected, our own needs, just like our own foot, must also receive attention and resources. What are our needs? We have physical needs for sleep, healthy food, and exercise. We have social and emotional needs for intimacy and connection. We have spiritual needs for meaning and purpose. We have intellectual needs for learning, stimulation, and growth. And when we attend to our own needs, to all the important pieces of our life mosaic, we can be in greater service to the whole, because we will be stronger. We will also be happier and, let's face it, a lot more fun to be around. Martyrs are not known for being the life of the party!

I'll close with a final example about trees. I've always loved trees, and during the pandemic shutdown, I spent as much time in the woods as I could. In the summer of 2020, I also read *The Overstory* by Richard Powers. It's a beautifully written book, with one character I loved, named Dr. Patricia Westerford. I was so engrossed in her storyline and the work that she did, including the description of the book she wrote, that I pulled out my phone to try to find her book online. You can imagine my disappointment when I sheepishly remembered that she was a fictional character, and therefore I could *not* actually read her book.

However, about a year later (thanks to my sister Becky, incredible bibliophile and scholar), I discovered that Dr. Patricia Westerford was based on a *real* ecologist, Suzanne Simard, and that Simard had a book I *could* read! I was beyond thrilled.

Simard's book, *Finding the Mother Tree*, tells her story as a silviculturist and researcher, starting with her early jobs in the forestry service of British Columbia. She tells about her job of replanting forests after clear-cutting, and the prevailing wisdom of the time. In essence, the belief was that trees could be farmed just like monoculture crops. To do that, the goal was to plant the most valuable trees and help them grow as quickly and strongly as possible. That meant clear-cutting and then replanting whatever species of tree was most valuable, regardless of what had been there before. It also meant a "free to grow" campaign, which sounds nice, but in reality meant poisoning all other vegetation in the area, so that the new seedlings would have less competition for light, water, and nutrients, and thus would be "free to grow."

Clearly this view of how a tree would grow was based on a fundamental paradigm of scarcity, which necessitates competition. Foresters believed wholeheartedly that trees and other forest vegetation stood alone, and that they competed for resources. Of course, when that is the paradigm, when survival of the fittest is the prevailing worldview, then the destruction of other life could be rationalized as being "for the greater good," or even necessary. It made me think of many other times, currently and throughout recorded history, that humans have stamped out cultures, other people groups, and even character traits, all the while rationalizing this oppression with a similar worldview: one that only recognizes winners, competition, and forceful domination.

But it turns out, that's *not* how a forest actually works! Simard speaks of her scientific discoveries, confirming ancient wisdom of Indigenous peoples, to show that trees and other forest vegetation work in cooperation with one another. She found this when seedling after replanted seedling failed to grow, despite their so-called "freedom." It turned out, the plants are deeply interdependent, using vast underground connections of roots and fungi forming a mycorrhizal network. In a healthy forest, trees are connected to each other and other vegetation using this network to share water and nutrients. Simard even speaks of how the elder trees, which she dubs the mother trees, send nutrients and sugar to younger saplings, which may not receive enough sunlight to photosynthesize adequately. Even when resources are scarce, the interdependence of the ecosystem allows the forest to be more, not less, resilient.

I believe the same is true for us and our human systems, that interdependence, and not just independence, makes us stronger.

So what does this mean? It means that our life mosaics are connected. That we never know, like the butterfly effect, where our influence will lead. It means that we can take care of ourselves while also taking care of our partners, our family members, our friends, and our neighbors. It means that when we come together as humans, we can create containers that support human development and thriving in our schools, churches, hospitals, and community centers—wherever we do the work that matters to us.

But it starts by checking in and seeing how well our work and our nonwork are supporting each other in our life mosaic.

By seeing if we are living our values and being good caretakers of ourselves. And by coming home to ourselves and to our lives with a process that will honor all of who we truly are: alignment.

Acknowledgments

I'VE ALWAYS BELIEVED that no one does big things alone. This book, certainly a "big thing" in my life, has been supported and influenced by so many people. In fact, I was tempted to skip an acknowledgments page, because first, I hope I've shared with folks what their support means to me, and second, I know I can't possibly include everyone here. Still, I have so much joy and gratitude to share.

I'm grateful to my teachers and mentors, including my parents (my first teachers, and still among my biggest supporters) and my Montessori mentors, especially Marta, Barb, Rosemary, and Susanne. I am also grateful to so many people (some of whom I have never met) but who nevertheless impacted my thinking about research and scholarship, adult development, and how to be of service to the world in a sustainable way.

I'm grateful to my Montessori students, both adolescent and adult, for sharing their lives with me. I have always learned as much from my students as I am sure they learned from me. To my CMStep team, thank you for partnering with me in our meaningful work and then also for the support in writing and thinking time away from that work to make this book possible.

I'm grateful to my two sisters, Becky and Abby, for their support and cheerleading, not only around this book, but for my whole life. And to all my other family members and dearest friends who have expressed interest, support, and confidence that this was an important message to share with the world.

I'm grateful for everyone who advised and sparred with me on my writing and ideas, believing in the value of this message. Thank you to my Montessori friends and colleagues, the Top Three team, my Sheroes Journey group, and to my HPS and RExer friends. I also owe special thanks to Jeffrey Shaw, Jennifer MacMillan, Rebecca Schinsky, Heather Gerker, Carol Gunn, Larry Kay, Joey Masiuk, and Edy Nathan, for conversations and connections that made this book better.

I'm grateful to all who supported this process of writing, to AJ Harper, who supported me from day one and believed that I could write a book that would change lives (even if it did take me over four years to go from a first draft of the fundamentals of this book to final publication), to Trena White and the Page Two team, who shepherded me through this process with kindness, support, grace, and finesse. A special thanks to my editors Kendra Ward, Rachelle Kanefsky, and Kelly Laycock, to my project managers Rony Ganon and Tass Barry, and to my designer Jen Lum. Each of you could not have been more helpful, more insightful, more professional, and this final product is due in no small part to your expertise and guidance. I'm only sorry I didn't come to you sooner!

And finally, I'm always grateful to Jonathan, my person, my partner. Thank you for always believing in and supporting my work, even (or especially) when I was out of alignment.

Notes

1: Work-Life Balance Is a Lie

p. 14   *a primary driver of clinical burnout*: Christina Maslach and Michael P. Leiter, "Understanding the Burnout Experience: Recent Research and Its Implications for Psychiatry," *World Psychiatry* 15, no. 2 (2016): 89–192, doi.org/10.1002/wps.20311.

p. 14   *noun:* alignment: OED.com, s.v. "alignment, noun," accessed March 13, 2021, oed.com/dictionary/alignment_n.

p. 19   *"A master in the art of living draws*: Lawrence Pearsall Jacks, *Education Through Recreation* (London: University of London Press, 1932), 1–2.

p. 21   *narrowing educational achievement gaps*: Angeline S. Lillard, Megan J. Heise, Eve M. Richey, Xin Tong, Alyssa Hart, and Paige M. Bray, "Montessori Preschool Elevates and Equalizes Child Outcomes: A Longitudinal Study," *Frontiers in Psychology* 8 (October 2017): 1783, doi.org/10.3389/fpsyg.2017.01783.

p. 21   *the brains of Montessori students*: Martin Schetter, David Romascano, Mathilde Gaujard, Christian Rummel, and Solange Denervaud, "Learning *by* Heart or *with* Heart: Brain Asymmetry Reflects Pedagogical Practices," *Brain Sciences* 13, no. 9 (2023): 1270, doi.org/10.3390/brainsci13091270.

p. 21 *significantly higher well-being scores*: Angeline S. Lillard, M. Joseph Meyer, Dermina Vasc, and Eren Fukuda, "An Association Between Montessori Education in Childhood and Adult Wellbeing," *Frontiers in Psychology* 12 (November 2021): 721943, doi.org/10.3389/fpsyg.2021.721943.

2: Let's Face It, Our Work Is Personal

p. 38 *thriving at work is positively correlated*: Gretchen Spreitzer, Christine L. Porath, and Cristina B. Gibson, "Toward Human Sustainability: How to Enable More Thriving at Work," *Organizational Dynamics* 41, no. 2 (2012): 155–62, doi.org/10.1016/j.orgdyn.2012.01.009.

p. 47 *Montessori's cosmic plan*: Camillo Grazzini, "Maria Montessori's Cosmic Vision, Cosmic Plan, and Cosmic Education," *NAMTA Journal* 38, no. 1 (Winter 2013): 107–16, eric.ed.gov/?id=EJ1078117.

p. 54 *"If it falls your lot to be a street sweeper*: Martin Luther King Jr., "What Is Your Life's Blueprint?" Speech at Barratt Junior High School, October 26, 1967, Philadelphia, PA, projects.seattletimes.com/mlk/words-blueprint.html.

3: You Don't Have to Quit Your Job

p. 62 *A 2017 review of literature on human thriving*: Daniel J. Brown, Rachel Arnold, David Fletcher, and Martyn Standage, "Human Thriving: A Conceptual Debate and Literature Review," *European Psychologist* 22, no. 3 (July 2017): 167–79, doi.org/10.1027/1016-9040/a000294.

p. 62 *Having this appropriate challenge level*: Richard M. Ryan and Edward L. Deci, *Self-Determination Theory: Basic Psychological Needs in Motivation, Development, and Wellness* (New York: Guilford Press, 2018).

p. 71 *"wherever you go, there you are"*: Jon Kabat-Zinn, *Wherever You Go, There You Are: Mindfulness Meditation in Everyday Life* (New York: Hyperion, 1994).

4: Finding Alignment, Part I

p. 83   *And now his work continues*: See chrisnortonfoundation.org.

p. 83   *"push past life's challenges"*: Chris Norton, "About," accessed January 20, 2025, chrisnorton.org/about.

p. 86   *if all other levels of needs can be met*: A.H. Maslow, "A Dynamic Theory of Human Motivation," in *Understanding Human Motivation*, edited by C.L. Stacey and M. DeMartino (Cleveland: Howard Allen Publishers, 1958), 26–47, doi.org/10.1037/11305-004.

p. 86   *three basic psychological needs*: Ryan and Deci, *Self-Determination Theory*.

p. 87   *Having these needs met in life is critical*: Brown et al., "Human Thriving."

p. 89   *mindfulness is "paying attention in a particular way*: Kabat-Zinn, *Wherever You Go, There You Are*, 4.

6: Expanding Your Mosaic

p. 118   *"Help me to do it alone" is the child's cry*: Maria Montessori, *From Childhood to Adolescence*, Montessori Series, vol. 12 (Amsterdam: Montessori-Pierson Publishing Company, 1948; 2014), 63.

p. 119   *the kind of learning that "fills the vessel"*: Eleanor Drago-Severson, *Leading Adult Learning: Supporting Adult Development in Our Schools* (Thousand Oaks, CA: Corwin Press, 2009).

p. 120   *"human beings are works in progress*: Daniel Gilbert, "The Psychology of Your Future Self," TED Talk, March 2014, 6 min., 35 sec., ted.com/talks/dan_gilbert_the_psychology_of_your_future_self.

p. 121   *fulfilling their own human potential*: Maslow, "A Dynamic Theory of Human Motivation."

p. 121   *"valorization of the personality"*: Montessori, *From Childhood to Adolescence*, 61.

p. 122   *Maslow described self-actualizing individuals*: A.H. Maslow, *Motivation and Personality* (New York: Harper & Row, 1954), 201, as cited in William C. Compton, "Self-Actualization Myths: What Did Maslow Really Say?" *Journal of Humanistic Psychology* 64, no. 5 (2024): 743–60, doi.org/10.1177/0022167818761929.

p. 122   *"Self-actualizing people are*: Abraham Maslow, "Self-Actualization and Beyond," proceedings paper, Conference on the Training of Counselors of Adults, Center for the Study of Liberal Education for Adults, Chatham, Massachusetts, May 22–28, 1965, 110.

p. 122   *Maslow's ideas are not without critics*: Ryan and Deci, *Self-Determination Theory*.

p. 122   *Research on thriving*: Brown et al., "Human Thriving."

7: Honoring Our Alignment

p. 138   *a study of mindfulness for teachers*: Patricia A. Jennings, Joshua L. Brown, Jennifer L. Frank, Sebrina Doyle, Yoonkyung Oh, Regin Davis, Damira Rasheed, Anna DeWeese, Anthony A. DeMauro, Heining Cham, and Mark T. Greenberg, "Impacts of the CARE for Teachers Program on Teachers' Social and Emotional Competence and Classroom Interactions," *Journal of Educational Psychology* 109, no. 7 (2017): 1010–28, createforeducation.org/wp-content/uploads/2020/06/Jennings-NYU-Study-ED-Psych-2017-published.pdf.

p. 139   *embrace the limits of what is possible*: Oliver Burkeman, *Four Thousand Weeks: Time Management for Mortals* (New York: Farrar, Straus and Giroux, 2021).

8: Our Ever-Changing Mosaics

p. 156   *Rights and responsibilities are also at the heart*: T.M. Scanlon, *What We Owe to Each Other* (Cambridge, MA: Belknap Press of Harvard University Press, 2000).

p. 156   *that's the point of the show, very explicitly*: Krystie Lee Yandoli, "'The Good Place' Creator Michael Schur Explained the Real Message of the Show," *BuzzFeed News*, November 21, 2019, buzzfeednews.com/article/krystieyandoli/the-good-place-michael-schur.

p. 157   *"eliminating things that harm us is not*: Shawn A. Ginwright, *The Four Pivots: Reimagining Justice, Reimagining Ourselves* (Berkeley, CA: North Atlantic Books, 2022), 7.

9: Your Alignment Matters

p. 159   *the deeper relationships she now forges*: Abby Keller Coaching, "Home," accessed January 20, 2025, abbykellercoaching.com.

p. 168   *the happiness of people to three degrees of separation*: James H. Fowler and Nicholas A. Christakis, "Dynamic Spread of Happiness in a Large Social Network: Longitudinal Analysis over 20 Years in the Framingham Heart Study," *BMJ* (2008): 337:a2338, doi.org/10.1136/bmj.a2338.

p. 168   *"help me to do it alone"*: Montessori, *From Childhood to Adolescence*, 63.

p. 169   *"that much is expected of them eventually*: Robin Wall Kimmerer, *Braiding Sweetgrass: Indigenous Wisdom, Scientific Knowledge, and the Teachings of Plants* (Minneapolis, MN: Milkweed Editions, 2013), 112.

p. 169   *"cultures of gratitude*: Kimmerer, *Braiding Sweetgrass*, 115.

About the Author

Tina Thomas

DR. KATIE KELLER WOOD grew up in the world of education, and she delights in helping people find new ways of thinking about the world. Discovering Montessori education, both as a pedagogy and a philosophy, was pivotal for her, and she is on a mission to bring a Montessori perspective of work to everyone.

Katie has had the great honor of working with hundreds of middle and high school Montessori teachers from all over the world through the training program she runs called CMStep. She is recognized as a leader in Montessori programming for adolescents and adults, and she is active in the Montessori research and teacher education communities.

Katie lives in Richmond, Virginia, and any given semester might find her teaching undergraduates at the University of Virginia (where she earned both her bachelor's and her doctorate), master's students at Purdue Fort Wayne, and/or doctoral students at the University of Wisconsin–River Falls. Katie is a TEDx and keynote speaker and a sought-after presenter for workshops and conferences.

Katie does her work because she believes that a more peaceful, just, equitable, and sustainable world is possible, and that it takes all of us leading our aligned lives to bring this world forward. *Alignment: A Montessori Approach to Reimagining Work-Life Balance* is her first book.

We Are Better Together!

Let's Stay in Touch

I'm honored to be a partner in your alignment journey. While our life's alignment is personal, it doesn't have to be private. I would love to stay in touch with you. Contact me through my website, katiekellerwood.com.

Speaking and Workshops

It has been my honor to serve audiences from seven to seven hundred, with workshops and presentations that range from fifteen minutes to five days. Let's chat to see if I would be the right fit for your next workshop, Zoom gathering, conference, or retreat. You can also join my email list at katiekellerwood.com to stay up to date on what I'm offering and where I'll be presenting.

Copies for Your Organization

If you're ready to bring *Alignment* to others, whether that be your team, your book group, or even your friends and family, please contact me! Discounts for bulk orders are available, and I'd love to make your copies extra special.

A Favor

If you have gotten value from *Alignment*, will you please take a minute or two to write a review? In our interconnected world, your review can help bring others closer to their own alignment. Thank you for helping me with my purpose work, too.